David,

You have been a wonderful friend over the past two years. I wish you the best of luck in the future. I know that you will be very successful at whatever you do. I'll never forget the times we shared.

Love,
Heather Seal

BRINGING BACK THE BAY

Sitting on the pier by Davis Creek, Bavon, Virginia, 1993

I don't think it matters whether it's true or not If you're collecting stories you're going to get embellishments. My job is simply to present the information as it's given. These are stories passed down one to the other. Embellishment is what oral history is all about. That's part of the problem with the Chesapeake. Not much was written about it, when you look at the scope of it and how long it's been around. So we have to write down what's available to us. We don't have to accept it as the gospel truth. LARRY CHOWNING

ENDPAPERS:
Rhode River, 1959

Bringing Back the Bay

The Chesapeake in the
Photographs of Marion E. Warren
and the Voices of Its People

Marion F. Warren

MARION E. WARREN

with Mame Warren

THE JOHNS HOPKINS UNIVERSITY PRESS

Baltimore and London

1994

Contents

This book has been brought to publication with the generous assistance of the National Endowment for the Humanities and the Maryland Humanities Council.

THE JOHNS HOPKINS UNIVERSITY PRESS
2715 North Charles Street
Baltimore, Maryland 21218-4319
The Johns Hopkins Press Ltd., London

ISBN 0-8018-4906-3

Library of Congress Cataloging-in-Publication Data will be found at the end of this book.
A catalog record for this book is available from the British Library.

The Chesapeake Bay Bridge, 1953

I can't say, over the miles, that I had learned what I had
wanted to know because I hadn't known what I wanted to
know. But I *did* learn what I didn't know I wanted to know.

—William Least Heat Moon, *Blue Highways*

We acknowledge permission from Little, Brown and Company to
quote from *Blue Highways* by William Least Heat Moon.

To Aunt Edna, who believed in me and aimed me in the
   right direction

To Carleton Mitchell, whose demand for perfection pushed
   me to be a fine printer

To Mary Giblin Warren, my wife of fifty years, whose
   support and loyalty have made my career a pleasure

MEW

To Henry Holladay Harris, who makes it all possible

MW

Steward Shipyard archaeological dig near Shady Side, Maryland, 1993

*If you want to know how ordinary people lived, then you want to know what kept them alive or
killed them off. From archaeology we learn a great deal about shelter and diet. It's from archaeology
that we learned that housing in the Chesapeake was almost entirely impermanent, unlike
New England. There are hundreds of documented seventeenth-century houses still standing in New
England; so far, in Maryland, we have only one residence. In Virginia, there are one or two.*

*They used post-in-the-ground architecture, and termites got in; they used clapboard roofs, and
they leaked like mad so they rotted from the top; if they sealed them with tar, they burned down.
That style of impermanent architecture lasted well into the eighteenth century, though with the
appearance of a primarily adult native population, they had the time and resources to build more
permanent housing. But in the seventeenth century, life was so short that by the time a man
wanted to do that, he was likely to die.* LOIS GREEN CARR

Preface

BRINGING BACK THE BAY strives to achieve two goals: to provide a reflection of the Chesapeake Bay's past and present and to intimate the possibility of its renewal. Readers will, we hope, see beyond the skipjacks, yachts, and speedboats. As we survey the communities that have evolved along the Bay and its tributaries, the faces and voices on these pages form a living mosaic of the Chesapeake in the last half of the twentieth century.

Because I was born here, I take the uniqueness of the Bay and its way of life for granted, but my father never has. He was born in Montana in 1920, grew up on farms in rural Missouri, and attended high school and began his photographic career in St. Louis. So coming to Maryland in 1947 and spending time on and near so much water was new and fascinating to him.

I often joke that as a child I thought we needed passports to cross the state line, so seldom did our family leave Maryland. We rarely stayed home, however. Every weekend we were off exploring some obscure community, traveling back roads that seemed to lead nowhere, but they always offered a picture opportunity when we stopped. It is no coincidence that the numbering system my parents established for my father's stock photography files was titled Maryland Illustrated.

Thomas Point light, c. 1970

Nearly a half-century of documenting the Chesapeake Bay region convinced Marion Warren that photographs can make a difference in how we perceive the history of everyday life. This realization, combined with his growing concern about the threatened condition of the Chesapeake Bay's ecology, provided the catalyst for this book. And so, in late 1984, my father set out to save the Bay with his camera. He dubbed his enterprise the Bay Project. He attended hearings and conferences, joined committees, and lobbied legislators. Most of all, he listened and learned about subjects that had nothing to do with photography.

Marion Warren's midwestern roots are evident in his expansive definition of the Chesapeake Bay and its environs; he unabashedly includes 4-H competitions and church socials, county fairs and country stores in his visual journal. Anything and everyone that touch the Bay have an impact, he reasons, and are part of the story. He is attracted especially to working people: watermen and their families, crab pickers, farmers, school teachers, store keepers, migrant workers, and the Native Americans whose ancestors were the first to reap the bounty of the Bay.

We debated for quite a while whether to produce his Bay Project in black and white or in color. We had long conversations about the benefits and drawbacks of each. Color, he argued, is what people want and expect today. It had been his concentration for more than twenty years. But black-and-white photographs, we both knew, have greater archival value—meaning that, if properly processed, they are not subject to fading, as color images often are. What settled the controversy was his realization that you can read so much more into a photograph when you are not distracted by color. Besides, taking the photograph is only about ten percent of the pleasure he gets from his profession. What he really enjoys is hunkering down in the darkroom and discovering the full potential of a negative.

For many years my mother (and then numerous other assistants) worked with my father to maintain order among the more than one hundred thousand negatives he has created. Together, they established his reputation, first through a commercial studio, then later at their gallery in Annapolis. In 1987 my parents turned over the day-to-day management of the collection to the Maryland State Archives (where I am curator of photographs), and my father was free to pursue his Bay Project virtually full time. Three years later I published *Then Again . . . Annapolis, 1900–1965,* a book of photographs with text drawn from oral history interviews with long-time residents of my home town. My father read the book and recognized the potential of its format for his Bay book. He urged me to join his Bay Project, and in 1992 I signed on.

Over the next year and a half we traveled extensively in the Chesapeake watershed, sometimes together, sometimes separately. My father was laden with cameras, lenses, tripods, filmholders (entirely too much stuff for a seventy-three-year-old man to lug alone). I packed light: a professional Sony tape recorder, two external microphones, and lots of blank cassettes. Usually we went off on two- or three-day trips in his trusty van (so that he could climb on its roof when he needed extra height to take pictures). These excursions enhanced my appreciation for the challenge Marion Warren had set for himself. At a time in life when most people are settling into a comfortable retirement, my father chose to stretch himself and his art so that our vision, and posterity's, could be expanded.

Interviews were sometimes carefully arranged and prepared for, but just as often, they were spontaneous. One drizzly morning in Deltaville, Virginia, for instance, we encountered Skipper Garrett and Willis Wilson by chance at a marine railway. Skipper gave me only a few choice minutes of taping, but Willis sat down by the wood stove and reminisced for more than an hour. From there, we hurried to our scheduled appointment with Larry Chowning in nearby Urbanna.

I was particularly interested in uncovering the role women have played on and around the Chesapeake. While my father haunted the piers and peeler sheds, I settled down at kitchen tables and listened to what it means to provide support for a husband who leaves at five in the morning and returns twelve hours later with bushels of busters that need tending. The concern of the women for their husbands' safety and their devotion to their families were as palpable as the crabcakes they molded with their overworked hands.

Matching appropriate quotations with photographs was the most satisfying component of my work. Sometimes, even as someone was answering a question, I knew which photograph that quote would appear with. At other times, my father took the photograph as I conducted the interview. Interviewees often revealed themselves to be homespun scholars who grasped not only the immediacy of their own experiences but also the broader implications for a threatened culture. Jennings Evans lamented the decline of gatherings at country stores, and his colloquial phrasing inspired our title, "Bringing Back the Bay":

> *The hot stove is kind of dwindling away now. That's something we miss. That's where everybody gathers at nighttime to tell stories after a day of crabbing. Conversations are spontaneous. It kind of starts and drifts from one subject to another, and it all depends on the mood of the particular gang there. Sometimes they got the impotence in them and they're kind of mean-spirited. Other times, things are going good and they start telling these jokes.*
>
> *They'd lean back in their chairs, "Oh, I remember one time, how it was then." That's what it is, it's bringing back the past; it keeps the past alive for the old people, to tell their experiences to the younger ones and tell them how they had it.*

The text that appears with the photographs has been edited only for clarity. The richness of vocabulary and variety of speech patterns have, I hope, been preserved. Readers should be aware that the spoken word has little in common with carefully composed prose. My intent is to convey a clear impression of the individual expressing personal experiences and convictions. For those who wish to know more about the persons behind the voices, a list of narrators with brief biographical notes appears in the back of the book.

Captions are deliberately minimal. If Marion Warren had his way, there would be no captions at all; he wants the photographs to speak for themselves. Everyone else involved in organizing the book—our publisher, editors, designer, and I—felt that this would be unfair to the reader. We insisted on providing at least the location and year the picture was taken, with a brief explanation of the activity depicted if it is not self-explanatory. Those curious to know more will find ample detail in the commentaries, including the exact date of the photograph, if known. The dates are particularly interesting because they sometimes reveal how many striking images Marion Warren can take in just a few days' time. A good example is his first excursion to Smith Island in July 1965 or his return trips there in 1991 and 1992. Accession numbers that follow each caption refer to the Maryland State Archives' cataloging system for the Marion E. Warren Collection.

The predominant voice in the book is Marion Warren's. Each chapter begins with an essay in which he explains why he clustered that particular group of photographs together and draws some conclusions from his long experience on the

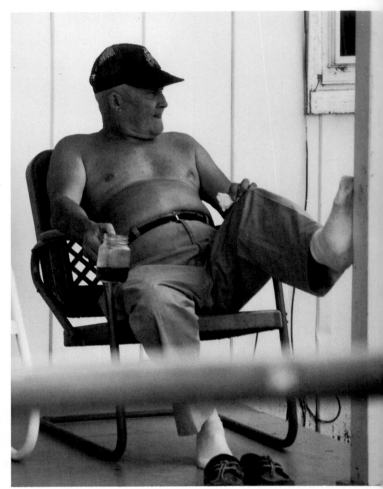

Bay. The essays were distilled from many hours of tape-recorded conversation about when, where, how, and why he took every photograph that appears in this volume. The Photographer's Commentaries at the back of the book are a rich lode of information for aspiring (as well as accomplished) photographers because my father shares all sorts of tricks he has learned over the years. More important, they include thoughtful analysis of the people and situations he has encountered, and his reasons for including these subjects as illustrations of the Chesapeake Bay and its watershed.

Bringing Back the Bay is, I think, three books in one. For those who simply want a handsome picture book, it is here, though there also are some harsh images of threatened aspects of the Chesapeake. It also presents an opportunity to become better acquainted with the people who live and work by the Bay through images that illustrate pride in their labor and their heritage even as their words convey concern for the future of the Bay. And for those who want to know more about the man behind the camera, Marion Warren's own thoughts introduce us to the mind of a master photographer—an artist devoted to his profession, and his subject.

MAME WARREN

Acknowledgments

Many people have contributed to the Bay Project in countless ways over the last ten years. To every person who paused long enough to let Marion's camera or Mame's recorder capture a part of him or herself, we are most grateful. To all those who answered questions, offered support, or reinforced our enthusiasm for this project, we express our appreciation.

Generous sponsorship for this effort has come from numerous sources. Early benefactors include the late Elizabeth Myer Mitchell, the Chesapeake and Potomac Telephone Company of Maryland, and the Chesapeake Bay Trust. We are also grateful to the Maryland Humanities Council, the National Endowment for the Humanities, and the Robert G. Merrick Foundation for their sponsorship of a lecture series that helped us to determine areas of general interest and concern about the Bay.

Advocates of the Bay Project came from various quarters: Will Baker, Rod Coggin, and especially John Page Williams at the Chesapeake Bay Foundation; Elaine Eff of the Cultural Conservation Program of the Maryland Department of Housing and Community Development; Thomas W. Burke Jr. of the Chesapeake Bay Communications Office under Governor William Donald Schaefer. Special thanks go to Andrea Hammer, who encouraged us to find the essential ideas in the interviews, and to Tom Horton, whose thoughtful suggestions have guided our approach to the Bay.

As the home of the Marion E. Warren Collection, the Maryland State Archives provided gracious hospitality. State Archivist Edward C. Papenfuse offered a rearrangement of Mame's schedule as curator of photographs that permitted her to participate more actively in the book's production. On Tuesdays, volunteers Marguerite Smith, Helen Orme, Gladys Lambert, Harrison Sayre, and Greg Halpin struggled to keep up with the deluge of new negatives and prints to be accessioned. Time and again, we spread hundreds of photographs on the Archives' conference tables as we winnowed selections for this volume.

Getting out on the Bay is sometimes a challenge for those of us unwilling to accept the responsibility of owning a boat. Several people offered outings on the water and revealed their favorite haunts to Marion and his lens: Dave Bausell; Paul Smith; Robbie Robinson; Mike Reber; Debbie Wilson and her late husband, Jim; and the late Ray Nash.

Gene Cronin has been almost a godfather to this project, from granting us an extraordinarily insightful and instructive interview to accompanying us on a particularly fruitful visit to Smith Island. Having Gene along assured that doors were opened with enthusiasm and wide smiles. On that same trip, Mike Harrison helped us identify Smith Islanders who appear in the photographs.

Fred Hecklinger pondered every picture of Chesapeake Bay craft and made sure that we could tell a bugeye from a buy boat (and even an occasional bugeye that *was* a buy boat). Careful reading of various sections of the manuscript prompted perceptive comments and corrections from John Page Williams, Greg Stiverson, Marguerite Smith, Gladys Lambert, Helen Orme, and, again, Gene Cronin.

Most important, of course, were those who participated in the interviews. Often humorous, sometimes harmonious, occasionally cacophonous, their voices form a multifaceted chorus. Thanks to Audrey Adams, Dave Bausell, Reuben Becker, Bobby Campbell, Lois Green Carr, Larry Chowning, Raymond Copper, Tommy Courtney, Gene Cronin, Downes Curtis, Marge Dowsett, Jennings Evans, Virginia Evans, Rockwood Foster, Bernie Fowler, Skipper Garrett, Bernard Gessner, Adrien Hansen, Walter Harris, Edward and Ella Harrison, Fred Hecklinger, Theodore Johnson, Brenda Harrison Marsh, Larry Marsh, Janice Marshall, Marian and Bobby McKay, Madison Mitchell, Pip Moyer, Suzanne Pogell, Etta Richwine, Robbie Robinson, Paul Smith, Anthony Thomas, Hazel Turner, Otis Turner, Sharie Valerio, Harvey Walters, John Page Williams, and Willis Wilson for the time they spent chanting the joys and sorrows of living by the Bay then and now.

Vince Leggett joined us on some outings and steered us to several memorable narrators. Some of the text on these pages was taken from interviews made in 1990 by Sharie Valerio, Beth Whaley, and Mame Warren as part of The Annapolis I Remember project.

Deborah Reid supplied invaluable encouragement along with flawless transcriptions of dozens of taped interviews. Her vivacious letters that accompanied each package persuaded us that our efforts, particularly the many hours of interviews with Marion, might indeed find an audience.

The staff of the Johns Hopkins University Press has championed this scheme virtually since its inception. In particular, Jack Goellner never wavered in his determination to see this volume in print. He provided abundant moral and technical support, and Bob Brugger guided us with a deft but light touch, for which we are grateful.

Jane McWilliams scrutinized every word on these pages with a sharp eye and sharper pencil. It is she we must thank for rescuing all of us from pointless prattling and needless repetition, particularly in the Photographer's Commentaries. Her gentle prodding and probing nudged us toward precision and clarity.

We are indebted to master designer Gerry Valerio for his ability to transfer from the mind's eye to the printed page the book Marion envisioned. With a keen sense of counterpoint, Gerry melds images and ideas into music harmonious to both eye and ear.

Finally, we acknowledge with love and gratitude the constant enthusiasm of our mates, Mary Giblin Warren and Henry Holladay Harris. Every time we returned from wandering the Chesapeake, they were waiting with a warm embrace and a willingness to listen to our adventures. No wonder it is always a joy to return to home port.

As we go to press, additional generous support for Bringing Back the Bay *was received from the Chesapeake Bay Program, a unique partnership among the states of Maryland, Virginia, and Pennsylvania; the District of Columbia; the Chesapeake Bay Commission, a tri-state legislative body; the U.S. Environmental Protection Agency, representing the federal government; and participating citizen advisory groups.*

BRINGING BACK THE BAY

Crab potter Bill White on the James River. 1993

When you go on the water, it's not like farming a field. A field is yours. This water out here belongs to everybody, so you can't have your own little place. So it's really not much good in worrying about it. You just have to get what you can get. BOBBY MC KAY

Them Days

Coming from the Midwest and growing up on a farm, I had never seen a body of water the size of the Chesapeake Bay. I suddenly saw pictures everywhere. If I'd grown up on the Chesapeake, I probably wouldn't have taken photographs with the fresh approach that I had just arriving. I photographed everything in sight because it had a newness for me. Now some of these views have become part of history because so much has changed.

I quickly realized I knew nothing about boating. I didn't know port from starboard or fore from aft. So the first winter I was here I took a Power Squadron course in basic navigation. I did it to be able to talk to the people on the Bay, to have a working knowledge of the terminology, not to learn to sail.

The first few years, I spent a great deal of time on the water, mostly sailing with faculty at the Naval Academy. It was a wonderful way to enjoy the Bay because the academy provided the boat and I was just along for the ride. I always announced to my captain that he should not count on me for any help, because the times I would have been needed were the times I most wanted to take photographs. I was just a little ballast for the boat. I liked sailing, but it was really just a form of transportation for me. It's sort of ironic, since they all grew up in Annapolis, that of our three children, only our son Paul became a really avid sailor.

When out on the water, I was always looking at the shoreline or watching other boats go past. I became fascinated with the seafood industry. After all, a sailboat can be very pretty, but it doesn't hold a candle to a skipjack as far as beauty is concerned. Those wooden boats with their stained sails and dredges hauling up oysters are about as photogenic as you can get. Then in the summer I discovered the astonishing blue crab, as challenging to eat as it is to catch.

While the skipjacks and tonging boats were completely new to me, the people who worked on them seemed very familiar. They were the same kind of people I had known from my childhood on the farm, only these men were harvesting seafood instead of crops. They both worked with nature, whether it be the water or the ground. It was very easy for me to listen to the watermen and learn about the Bay. Even today, as I talk to both watermen and farmers, they're basically the same people, they just do things a little differently.

Cove Point, Maryland, 1948

I love going by Thomas Point lighthouse because I like to think about that old lighthouse keeper in there a hundred years ago. I just feel nostalgic about it. I like to think of the life out there, living by your little dory or whatever kind of boat you used to get to shore with. HARVEY WALTERS

Lighthouse keeper, Cove Point, Maryland, 1948

Back there in them days, it was a whole lot colder. Many a time when we got through working out there on the Bay, my coat got damp and froze on me and I had to pull it off. Then at night when we'd go in the bunk, frost was all on top, and I had to go crawl under there and go to sleep. That would last a month or so at a time.

I've had it another time when we were up off the Patuxent River dredging and it come up a gale of wind. One of them heavy fogs come off the shore. And one of the fellows, he's still living down at Rhodes Point now, was on a skipjack. The fog hit into her and capsized her.

We were off running a little ways there, and we seen them. We sailed up back to them, and I got out in the rowboat there and went down and picked them up. There were five head of them aboard, holding onto the mast there, and I got ahold of them. But the last one, he give up. The others, they helped theirselves and I could pull them over in the boat. But that last one, he had give up nearly, and I tried pulling him over. I got him twice, and he slacked up. I seen nothing but he was going to drown right there in front of my eyes. But finally, I got ahold of him enough, and I pulled him on over into the rowboat.

One of the boys took the line of the boat and held on there and lifted them out and got them on the skipjack. He's dead now, but one or two of the fellows down at Rhodes Point is still living that was on there. EDWARD HARRISON

Oyster dredging,
Chesapeake Bay,
1954

Waterman's gloves, Wynne, Maryland, 1992

Not everybody could adjust to that cold. That's cold out there on them decks. I know, I've done it. Unless you know how to take care of the cold, you can near about freeze to death. Your hands get so numb sometimes, then you start beating them, then they'll come back and you'll be all right the rest of the day. But you have to let them get numb like that or you can't stand it. If you don't let them get numb, you'll be pestered all day. There's ways to handle the cold and you have to learn that.

Oystermen used to have to wear gloves that would cost ten cents, and they'd make two or three licks for the oysters and then they'd have holes in them, and there was nothing protecting them from the cold. They used to have to crank the dredges in, two men on each crank—four men in some cases on the schooners. Two would be on this handle, and two facing the other way on the other half. They had to pull in all those shells and all those oysters. Sometimes they'd hit a hang, and those things would get to spinning and crack their knuckles and break their arms. JENNINGS EVANS

Way back when my father was a'dredging, when they would leave in the fall, they wouldn't come home until Thanksgiving if it was pretty weather. If it was bad weather, they'd have to stay until Christmas.

Thanksgiving wasn't anything special. But Christmas, oh my! When they're expecting all the men home there's four and five cakes, chickens and ducks—you name it, they had it. Everything was decorated, lit up like I don't know what. They'd always stay 'til after New Year's and then they'd go back and stay out until March. VIRGINIA EVANS

Dredging oysters from a schooner, c. 1955

PREVIOUS SPREAD:
Drifting dredgers, Chesapeake Bay, 1956

8

The dredge was originally introduced to Chesapeake Bay in about 1820 by New Englanders who came down here. They'd exhausted the oyster supply up around Cape Cod, and they came here and started buying oysters. Right after the Civil War, dredging was made legal in Maryland waters, but only from a sailing craft. That law still stands, and that's why we have these skipjacks that are still working for a living. FRED HECKLINGER

FOLLOWING SPREAD:
Oyster tongers, Chester River, 1986

City Dock, Annapolis,
Maryland, 1950

There were a lot of oyster boats out in the harbor. In the wintertime one man, I think, did freeze to death over there because it got so cold. They'd go oystering and then many times they'd get iced in. And they didn't have any plumbing or anything. Of course, it all went into the creek. Lovely. We were not permitted to go over on the dock after dark, or anywhere near dark actually, because there were so many saloons over there. MARGARET MOSS DOWSETT

I'd tell them in the beginning there was no drinking allowed on that boat when we were out on that Bay working. I said, "On the weekend, that's your business. You do what you want. But you ain't going to do it aboard this boat." And we always had a good crew.

And another thing. Wherever we harbored, we'd tell them not to bother nothing where we tied up at, and we never had a complaint in our life. Up to Annapolis there, we'd go in there and tie up to the docks there, and they were dealing there in the grocery stores and everything, and we never had a complaint with a man in our life while we owned that skipjack. EDWARD HARRISON

Unloading oysters, Solomons Island,
Maryland, c. 1960

*It seems like a dream, remembering
how all these people would get down
there and shovel the oysters out and
throw them up on the pile. Boy,
there's a lot of activity to an oyster.
Everybody working just as hard as
they could go. Now you go over there,
you never see any of that anymore.
That's why I say, it's like a dream.
And not a lot of oysters is caught. It
seems like you never seen anybody
taking them out. They come by truck,
most of them, because our supply's just
about played out. This disease won't
let up, this MSX.*
JENNINGS EVANS

*When I began to work on the Bay in
the forties, there was a sense of abun-
dance and plenty, and oysters anywhere you wanted to pick them up on
the bottom, and they're just all gone.
The little perch around the pier aren't
even there like they used to be. Of
course, the grasses are not there like
they were. Just tremendous change and
loss. New people coming in who walk
out on that pier don't expect to see
small fish in the water and don't expect to catch bluefish.*
GENE CRONIN

Oyster bounty, Annapolis,
Maryland, c. 1948

City Dock, Annapolis,
Maryland, 1949

One thing that happens when you're raised in Annapolis is that the water becomes a part of your visual and spiritual being. You take it for granted that you will see water every day of your life probably, if you're an Annapolitan and you go out.

And I didn't know that that was part of me. I didn't get it until I went to Ohio with my husband to visit in-laws and I got claustrophobic, and I really didn't know what was the matter with me. We were there for a week, and about two or three days into the week, I said, "Where's the water? Isn't there any water around here? Is there a lake or something?" And I realized that I'm not used to that. And going across the Eastport bridge or the Weems Creek bridge, Severn River bridge, every day of my life, all my life, I'm used to that, and I think that gives you a wonderful sense, you know. It's a beautiful thing to have as a part of your inner self. SHARIE LACEY VALERIO

When I was a boy, two men could go out on a tong boat and catch thirty, forty bushels a day, and if they were real good and struck it good, they could catch as many as sixty bushel a day. These oystermen don't get sixty bushel in a week in the dredge boats, hardly, today. I could go right here in the City Dock or down at the foot of Prince George Street, even after World War II, and in a couple of hours, catch a bushel of crabs. I could stand down there a week now and couldn't catch a bushel of crabs. BOBBY CAMPBELL

Annapolis, Maryland, from Eastport, 1949

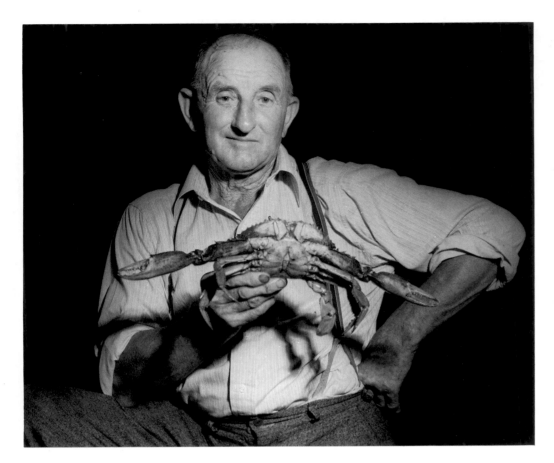

Capt. George Hallock
and his monster crab,
Whitehall Creek, near Annapolis,
Maryland, c. 1950

Male hard crabs, the biggest kind, like they're catching now, we used to get two dollars a barrel for them. Old fellow right across from the dock here had a crab house. He'd put them in these floats and ship them crabs to Chicago. He paid us crabbers two dollars a barrel, and we'd be glad to get that so we'd get rid of them. EDWARD HARRISON

The state law then was fifteen pounds. Anything over fifteen pounds had to be returned back to the Bay. Now, when rockfish season comes back in October, it'll be from eighteen inches to thirty-six inches that you can keep. By modern technology they found out that the younger fish would have a lot of eggs in them, too. They're more like, not to be derogatory, they're more like a younger woman. They will produce a stronger quality egg than would an older.

    I like a big rockfish, about five or six pounds, where I can take and clean him up, and it's a good meal for me for two or three times. You bake them with taters and onions like that for a couple hours at about 350, and it makes a real nice meal. I'd say a four- or five-pound rockfish to me is better, like I bake it. ROBBIE ROBINSON

Rockfish party,
near Annapolis, Maryland,
c. 1952

PREVIOUS SPREAD:
Crisfield, Maryland, c. 1957

18

Peeler shanty, Smith Island, Maryland, 1965

The only way a crab can grow is to throw off its old shell and develop a new skin which evolves into shell. As it approaches that shedding, there are signs that any good waterman can spot, particularly in the swimming paddle, a little red line develops in there. It's a new shell under the old one that you can see the edge of. The bottom part becomes yellowish. Eventually there is a crack developing under each side, and it begins to lift that old shell at the back—to back out of it. When it does, it's called a buster. A buster has started the shedding process. If you leave it in the water, that's an unstoppable process. If you take it out, it stops. It kind of freezes where it is, but the crab has difficulty in breathing, and it won't live very long. If you keep it in the water, it must begin this whole magnificent, miraculous process, pulling everything out of the old shell, all of its facial structure, the lining of its stomach, the covers of its gills, and all the external stuff, pulling that out of the old shell, and then absorbing chemicals from the water in for its own reserve to build up the beginnings of a new shell.

These were the simplest, neatest cooperatives I ever saw, because during the winter, half a dozen crabbers would get together and decide, "We'll run a shanty." They would own it collectively, usually. They would pay some old-timer to sit there and sort the peelers they brought in. They would bring all of their crabs to that shanty and turn them over to him. He would sort them and take out the soft crabs—not too soon, because they're fragile—and pack them up in sea grass, and take care of the shipping. At the end of the season, they would whack up the money, and the cooperative would disappear. I don't even know that they ever wrote a document. They all lived in the same community, and they all understood. There were probably twenty cooperatives on Smith Island. I don't know how many around Crisfield, maybe as many—Deal Island, places like that.

GENE CRONIN

Sorting peelers, Smith Island, Maryland, 1965

One of the fellows down on Deal Island has a sign on his pier says Stay Out, because he doesn't want people in there poking around his crabs. He has a sign a little bit farther out says No Trespassing. He has a sign on the door to his shanty that says Keep Out! This Means You! Some guy got on the pier, walked straight out there, walked in the shanty. And the guy in the shanty looked up; he says, "I bet you went to night school." The guy says, "Why do you think I went to night school?" He says, "You sure as hell can't read in the daylight." GENE CRONIN

General store, Ewell,
Maryland, 1965

I went to Smith Island before television, and every night, every man—all the watermen—no kids, no females, went to the stores. There were about three rows of benches, and each one of them had his regular place. They'd come in and they'd sit. They might buy a bottle of pop—not much more—and talk. And it was absolutely a wonderful place to hear the culture. They'd tell the same stories over and over and over again. You could see who were the respected people when they spoke, and who was laughed at by the group. You'd see kids come in—young men—and very quietly work their way into the group. They weren't very aggressive about it because the old-timers would cut them down. You could feel that culture as it existed at that time.

Then the first television set came, and it was put in the store by the storekeeper. Then they sat there and looked at that damn box, and didn't talk. And as time went on, they got television sets in their own house; they don't go to the store anymore. And I always remembered that change as one that was just a phasing-out of a center of culture to really nothing. I mean, television is no substitute at all. It's just a blah as far as personal relationships and community relationships and all the things that I enjoy. GENE CRONIN

Boardwalk, Smith Island, Maryland, 1965

Working the Water

Hand tonging for oysters
at the mouth of the
Severn River, c. 1953

After compiling *Maryland Time Exposures, 1840–1940*, I developed a sense of the kind of pictures that reach across the years and sustain a lasting impact. Clearly, the images that conveyed the strongest messages through time were those depicting people at work and at play in their natural surroundings. I realized that someone should be making that kind of record of the Chesapeake Bay region today, when so many seemingly permanent changes are taking place on so many different levels, especially among the people who make their living working on the Bay's waters.

With my knowledge of the Bay and its people, and my ability to do it, I felt that I was the obvious person to undertake the effort, so in 1985 I began what quickly became known as my Bay Project. I set out with my camera to record every aspect of life I could find that seemed apropos of the Bay region: native boats, farmers tilling the land, church gatherings, commerce in towns large and small. Time and again, though, I was drawn to remote places like Bennett Point, Wenona, Wynne, and Bavon, where the watermen come back season after season with their ever-diminishing catches. Those faces, young and old, were like magnets for my lens. They kept going out for the crabs, clams, oysters, and fish, and I kept going back to take their pictures.

Oystering on the Chesapeake is a way of life that seems to be disappearing fast. I can remember thirty years ago you'd find fifty hand-tong boats all working in close proximity on the oyster beds. Now you rarely see two or three at a time. There are two reasons: the diseases MSX and dermo have killed off most of the oysters, and secondly, it's a hard way to make a living. Not many people are willing to work that hard for so little return.

So that's why I'm out recording it all now while it's still here. The style of boat, how people stand, how close to shore they are (indicating where the oyster beds still are)—all of these things are vital information for future generations. I feel an urgency about getting it all on film not only because the industry is dying but also because I'm getting older, too. I know perfectly well that, like the oyster tongers, none of us will be around forever.

Andrew Wright,
Kent Narrows, Maryland,
1990

My father was a waterman. He had a deadrise skiff. It was about twenty-six feet long, or twenty-eight. And he worked in it, crabbed and oystered, both, out of it. I went out with him to cull the oysters, and he did the catching. Of course, I wasn't really big enough to handle the rakes, but when I got so I could handle the rakes, the oysters were plentiful and were heavy. When I first started, I could fill them but I didn't have success in boarding them because they were so heavy. But I finally did it.

It didn't look human to me for a man to have to do that. My father would go in the deep water where the oysters were old and big and hadn't been cut. And he'd get them out and some of them were, oh, six or seven inches long. DOWNES CURTIS

Have you ever seen oyster tongs? It all depends on where you're working. Some places out there are deeper than others. Some places you might have eighteen-feet tongs, some places you might have twenty-feet tongs. You've got to go out there and feel around until you get your right depth. And there's where you anchor until you can't catch no more oysters that day on that particular bed. Then you move on somewhere else. THEODORE JOHNSON

Culling oysters
on the Choptank River,
c. 1955

One thing about working on the water, the people are usually all equal. White folk and black folk are all equal. They're all doing the same thing. Oysters don't care who catches them. Nor do crabs. They'll come up for a black man as well as they will for a white man. So if a white man has more skills in catching oysters, he catches more. If a black man has more skills, then he catches more. And the man that catches more makes the better living.

The water business is an equal business. If a black man is out there in trouble and there's a white man who knows it, he'll help him. If there's a white man in trouble, the black man will help him. You get exactly what you make. If you make good, you have good. If you don't make good, then you don't. HAZEL T. TURNER

Oyster tongs, City Dock,
Annapolis, Maryland,
1987

Hand tonger at sunrise,
Tilghman Island, Maryland,
1987

The same type of guy is working the water down here in Virginia as works the water up there in Maryland. Hard-working, independent people that were brought up thinking, "That's what I'm supposed to do." If you're an oysterman hand tonging on Solomons Island and you're an oysterman hand tonging in Deltaville, Virginia, there are a few things you may be doing differently, but you're both doing the same thing. I don't see much difference. LARRY CHOWNING

Robbie Robinson,
Solomons, Maryland,
1992

Years ago, when I was tonging by myself, I could catch on the average anywheres from eight to ten, twelve bushel of oysters hand tonging. I have caught them high as seventeen bushel one day by myself—I struck a little oyster hill and it was nothing but clear oysters, but it was right in a doggone snowstorm, and I didn't stop. Snow was piling all over the place. You don't notice it when you're working like that. It's just the heat in your body keeps you warm. I've had icicles hanging on my beard. ROBBIE ROBINSON

Women never went on the river. After I got married—I was married when I was sixteen—one day I said to my husband, "I'll go with you. We can make more money."

I was not the first woman out there, but I was one of the first. And, boy, the first year I went out, those men had a fit when they saw me coming. "No place for a woman." "Can't go to the bathroom." "Why didn't you leave her home?" To see a woman out there was the most awful sight that any man had ever seen, and they didn't approve of it.

Well, rest assured, after seeing what I could do and the money that I was contributing, like I was another man helping him, then it was not too long before most of the men on the island had all their wives with them. AUDREY ADAMS

Bennett Point, Maryland, 1986

I might be completely wrong—I'm not a scientist—but I think we need a freeze-up. I think we need the whole Bay to freeze up. It seems like after a freeze-up, the oysters grow healthy for a while.

When we had snow and when we had ice, we had oysters, it seems like. Now with these warmer temperatures, it seems like it lets this MSX come on up the Bay on us nearly every year, and there's no let-up for these last few years.

They say snow does the land good in killing germs and all, so I don't know. It just might be a harebrained idea on my part, but I know one thing: When we don't have no freeze-up, we don't have no oysters.

JENNINGS EVANS

Robert L. Webster dredging oysters, c. 1953

Dredging oysters near the eastern
side of the Chesapeake Bay Bridge,
c. 1958

*Everything above this Bay bridge
seems to be living. Everything below
it, except around the Annapolis area,
even from Tilghman Island down,
even the mouth of the Choptank
River where your dredge boats used
to work, there isn't any oysters there.
The disease destroyed them; they're
gone. They can come back. It happened back in the fifties.*
ADRIEN HANSEN

Watermen at Kent Narrows,
Maryland, 1990

Peewee Bozman cooking aboard his workboat on Deep Creek, off the Magothy River, 1992

In my particular boat, I had two colored fellows with me, and one bunk stacked on top of the other, and I slept in the middle. We stayed right aboard there and cooked and ate the whole week. Then we'd head home Saturdays. I don't care about the weather, whether it was cloudy or raining, or whether foggy or blowing, whatever, we'd always come home on Saturday.

We'd never eat no crabs. It's too much trouble to cook them. Every once in a while we'd catch a flounder and we'd cook him. Sometimes we'd catch a rockfish; we'd have that. But our main food was bacon and eggs for breakfast, sometimes hot cakes and syrup, and for lunch we'd generally put a pot of soup on or a pot of beans or a clam chowder.

The man who was doing the cooking, he worked right on deck. He'd put this food on mornings when we were going out, and then he'd walk back every once in a while and look at it. And twelve o'clock come, I'd go eat, and they'd steer the boat and just pull the dredges along; and then after I'd eat, they'd go back and eat, and I'd steer and pull the dredges along. Then in between chances, they'd wash dishes. Then for supper, we'd have chicken, pork chops, steak—regular food—mashed potatoes, the whole caboodle. I did have one fellow, he always baked a cake. WILLIS WILSON

Why in the world anybody wants to be a waterman, I cannot see it. It's one of the worst jobs in the world, I told Willard and Bobby both. Do you know what they say? They're their own boss. I said, "Big deal. I'd rather have a boss than have to go out in that mess." I guess it makes them feel like they're doing something. It's up to them what they've earned over the years. I don't know what the appeal is. I can't see it. JANICE MARSHALL

Buy boats on the Magothy River
near the mouth of Deep Creek, 1969

At the end of the day you had to get in before dark. The buy boats were there, and you had to get in line and take your turn to put your oysters out. Sometimes I've seen as many as five and six buy boats. And if a new buy boat come in, you know he was going to pay more money.

Everybody got paid in cash every day. Some days you'd make thirty dollars, or some days you'd make twenty, and then some days you'd make a hundred dollars. Back then, that was a lot of money.

But the thing of it is, you didn't get going every day. You might go out once this week, or you might go out three days this week, and then for two more weeks, it might freeze up and you not get out at all. Sometimes the river would freeze over for two months and you couldn't work. By the time you got home and you paid your bills, you couldn't spend only so much of it because you didn't know when your next dollar was coming in. So it was like being a juggler. You had money in the air all the time, trying to make ends meet. But nobody went hungry. AUDREY ADAMS

Buy boat at City Dock, Annapolis, Maryland, 1992

It's very important that the seafood industry remain viable on the Chesapeake Bay. It is a gauge, a thermometer, to judge the health of the entire Bay. If we let the commercial seafood industry go we're going to lose that thermometer for all of us. We want people to be able to make a living on the water, to carry on a culture, a way of life. If we let it go, then we lose that gauge which is a way of looking at the Bay and saying it's getting healthier or it's not getting healthier. Who's going to get the oysters if we let the commercial end of it go? LARRY CHOWNING

35

Hard-shell clamming on
the James River, 1993

*On the Chesapeake Bay, it's funny.
When you're new, you're definitely an
outsider. You put in your time, and all
of a sudden you can do the same old
stupid things and it's not bad anymore. But when you're first doing it,
you're the entertainment for the old
guys.*

*I can remember the first day I went
clamming. I taught myself how to
clam. A few of the guys went down
and laughed a little bit, and one guy
finally came over and said, "Hey,
man, I can't stand it anymore. I've got
to show you how it's done."*
ANTHONY THOMAS

Soft-shell clamming operations near
Kent Island, Maryland, 1959

The people that used to oyster, they're going clamming. They use them same patent tongs, only heavier, for to catch clams with, and they're down the bottom. They take them heavy tongs that weigh two hundred pounds and dig them out. Sometime they catch one at a time, pull them up, sometime they catch three or four, sometime they catch five or six. Now they catch about eighteen hundred to two thousand a day of these little ones, and they're used for steamed clams.

WILLIS WILSON

Transporting clams,
c. 1960

When they invented the clam dredge and some of the oystermen, particularly over in Queen Anne's County, decided that that was going to tear up the oyster beds, there was close to war. You go over to Queen Anne's County towns where some clammers and some oystermen, they went to different gas stations, they went to different grocery stores. They really built up a tremendous antipathy and they would pour sugar into each other's gas tanks and ruin the engine or cut the boats loose. It was pretty serious for a while. But that died down.   GENE CRONIN

It's the old adage of the clammer. He goes out and catches three hundred dollars worth of clams, and the guy says, "You're catching too many clams. I got to drop the price." So what does the clammer do? The clammer goes out and catches more clams the next day to still make his three hundred dollars, so the price goes even lower. So he ends up catching more product for less and less money. If you go anywhere in the Bay, everybody says, "Overfishing, overfishing." But you have to do what you do to survive.   ANTHONY THOMAS

If you have a crab pot boat, you have to have this long, hard top canopy over the cockpit on which to stack these hundreds of crab pots when you set them out. You can't just stick them all in the cockpit; there's not enough room. During the winter, they may take that crab pot canopy off so they can rig the vessel for patent tonging, which requires a mast and a boom and some hydraulic equipment. FRED HECKLINGER

It's unbelievable, if you think about it, how the crabs keep coming. It's a powerful lot of crabs taken out of the water and so many crab pots, but still they keep coming. You'd think they would be gone, there's so many people after them. They hatch down at the mouth of the Bay, they say, where the water's saltier. This year there's been more what we call egg-bearing females— they have the orange sponge on them—than I've ever seen, and I didn't think when they finished this spring that they had left enough females out there to spawn.
BOBBY MC KAY

Crab potter Bill White
on the James River, 1993

Don Cawood and Keith Thomas, Deal Island, Maryland, 1988

The term waterman *goes back to England. A waterman on the Thames River was a man who worked a boat on the water. I don't ever remember hearing the term* waterman *used to represent a fisherman, crabber, oyster tonger, in any other place except the Chesapeake Bay. That's a Chesapeake Bay expression, and, I think, rather unique to the Chesapeake Bay watermen's culture.*
FRED HECKLINGER

Wooden boats are getting a little obsolete right now. The Jenkins Creek scraping boats are used for soft-shell crabs only. A long time ago they used them to catch oysters, because that's all they had. One boat did it all because they couldn't afford to have any other. LARRY MARSH

Crab scrape boat,
Rhodes Point, Smith Island,
Maryland, 1992

Repairing crab pots,
Wenona, Maryland, 1991

*You started crabbing in April. But
you had to get ready for crabbing. In
the wintertime, we would make crab
pots. We had a garage, and we'd sit
all night after we came in from work.
I would cook dinner, and we would go
out in the garage and make crab pots
until about ten o'clock. And then any
day that you were not working, you
were in the garage making crab pots
and preparing for the summer.*

*My husband would cut the wire
out and I would piece them together.
We'd make it into a square and put
four funnels into it and a partition.
The crabs went into the funnel and
then they went to a little trap and
then they laid into the top of the pot.
They couldn't get back down again
once they went up, because that's
where they would put the bait, in the
middle of the pot. Then we took the
lid off and dumped them out. I made
a couple hundred a year. We worked
all the time. We never stopped.*
AUDREY ADAMS

Crab pot floaters, St. Jerome's Creek,
1992

Joe Kitching, Smith Island,
Maryland, 1991

Crabbing is just like going to the office, essentially. As far as the time element, they go out at four or five o'clock in the morning and they're back at two o'clock in the afternoon. So it's better than going to the office. I think a lot of people working the water think it is. That's why they still do it. REUBEN BECKER

Crab skiff docking at Saxis, Virginia, 1989

Waterman keeping records, Saxis, Virginia, 1989

The legends should not be lost, but they should not be recited as fact. Everybody on Smith Island told me that on the first full moon in May we have a big shed of crabs. So I thought, well, I've got to get some better information, so I kept the daily records on about forty crabbers down there, forty scrapers going out for peelers. And the tricky thing was, the first year, they did. In seven years it never happened again, but they were still saying, "On the first full moon in May we always catch more." Well, the only good data I ever had says it's sometimes true.   GENE CRONIN

By "fooling with the crabs" I mean shedding the peelers. The ones that are the ripest we put in one float, and we put the busters in another float. And the green peelers that will not shed for like a week and a half, we put that in a separate float.

Then that's when my job comes in. I have to get up during the night and fish them every four hours, and you get out your busters and put them in a separate float and you get your soft ones out and you put them in the cooler. And I grade mine. I have a jumbo crab, which is usually five inches and over, and then the mediums are the smaller ones.

It's like a full-time job because you have to check the floats about every four hours, because once they turn soft, if you don't take them out of the water within a half an hour or so, they start a paper shell and they do their cycle again. Paper shell goes on back to a hard crab.

What I call a run of crabs is when he catches like two or three good bushels of peelers a day. Now I try to fish them around eleven o'clock and then when I get up at five-thirty. But when we do have the run, it is very tiring, I'll tell you. In the morning when I get up, I'm like a zombie.
MARIAN MC KAY

Tending shedding boxes, Taylor's Island, Maryland, c. 1987

Southern Maryland, c. 1957

I think that's one of the greatest fears a woman has, that something will happen to her husband on the water. You can pretty well accept illnesses, but when it's something that they love so well that takes their life. . . . I always heard my husband say that one of the greatest fears that a man has is becoming afraid of the water. But it's something you kind of want to put in the back of your mind. You know they're out there in storms, and there's nothing that you can do to help 'em except pray.

It's a hard life. You have to go like somebody's after you. It's a lot of long hours, a lot of tiring hours. You get up about three o'clock in the morning, and you get to bed maybe about eleven o'clock at night. A lot of times you'll put in eighteen to nineteen hours a day. That's day in, day out, except for Sunday. That's your day of rest and worship. BRENDA HARRISON MARSH

Sure you sail at night. You sail until you get to your destination. I brought ships down in fog, storms, all kinds of weather. And I tell you the truth; every time I go out in one of them big storms I would call on my Master. And Jesus piloted me home. Piloted me through all kinds of storms. OTIS TURNER

46

Bobby, Marian,
Gary, and Mark McKay,
Ridge, Maryland,
1992

My husband's father was a waterman, too. And then I have a son that is a waterman, that goes with his dad. He's twenty-five. So that's one, two, three generations.

I would like to see my son get a job, because I really think the water business is kind of going out. I think that in a few years we're not going to have the fish and the crabs if they don't take care of it. They're trying to save the Bay and all, but it's a long process.

But it's undependable, is what I'm saying. That's the reason why I feel like he should get a job that he knows what he's going to make each week. With this business, you never know what you're going to make. You have to budget yourself out, and you never know whether it's going to be a good winter or a bad winter. But he's happy doing it. You can't get it out of his blood, I guess is what it is. His dad did it and he likes it and he's happy doing it.

We've done fairly well. We had six kids. We've raised them. We own our own house now. We've had to work hard to get what we have, but it's been a good life. MARIAN MCKAY

If I've got a boat here and I say, "I need to stop because I'm catching too many little ones," I'm basically going to go out of business. So instead of doing that, I'm just going to keep scrapping and keep going and try to catch as many as I can, do whatever I can do, because I'm not going to just say, "Okay, I'm going out of business." You fight it to the end. ANTHONY THOMAS

Crab dredge boat, Davis Creek, 1993

Purdy Green's is probably one of the first boats that ever dredged for crabs in the Bay. Purdy was saying, "You know, we used to catch our limit every day, from the fifteenth of November until the first of April." But there weren't but eleven boats. I think last year they sold over five hundred dredge licenses. So you still got the same size pie; you're just cutting it up into a lot more different pieces, and there's not enough for everybody to survive.   ANTHONY THOMAS

The last dredged crabs of the season,
Bavon, Virginia, 1993

Steaming crabs, Pope's Creek,
Maryland, c. 1963

The people that have problems with crabmeat are the ones that are not willing to pay for the quality. Because there is a quality product there if you're willing to pay for it. I use lump crabmeat now. As a result, I have to put a little more money in the product to get a little more money out of it. I do not cut any corners and I will not allow the people who work for me to cut any corners. I look for a quality product all the time. RAYMOND COPPER

Crab pickers, Kent Island,
Maryland, 1963

One year I went up at Ewell and picked crabs. I'd get up at four o'clock in the morning and go up with a bunch of them. We'd have fun up there. First we'd be a'singing, then we'd be a'laughing and a'crying. We had a good time.

Someone would strike up a song and we'd all join in, whether it be a hymn, or another song, or what. I didn't no more mind getting up at four o'clock. I didn't mind it one bit in the world. I knew I was going to enjoy myself and make money, too.

I think they paid us twenty cents a pound. That's all we'd get. I wasn't very fast. There was one girl, she could pick twenty-five pounds in little or no time. I don't think I ever went over fifty for the day.
VIRGINIA EVANS

They tell you there's not an oyster in the Tred Avon now, in our river. The Bible says man is slowly eating himself up. Looks like it's true. And they're going to do the crabs the same way. They're just going to catch them all up until they pollute the survivors and there won't be enough to multiply.
DOWNES CURTIS

Capt. Elliot's crab-picking
operation, Grasonville,
Maryland, 1993

Capt. Bernard Hallock,
Shady Side, Maryland,
c. 1954

Papa was stern, but yet he was stern enough to learn us. He was trying to teach me something that he knew that I would have with me for the rest of my life, and I would never have to worry about it if I ever got married that I could feed my family with at all times. If I wanted to go to the water that would be fine, or if I wanted to work a job elsewheres, that would be fine. ROBBIE ROBINSON

Pound fishing, Shady Side,
Maryland, c. 1954

With pound fishing, you've got about ninety or a hundred poles you measure off and lay the net out. I have six nets out there. I check about three a day. I lose very few. Now the menhaden, they'll die off in a couple of days. You've got to fish them or turn them loose or something. You get the best catches about a half-hour after sundown when it's past the flood tide. They swim right into the net. TOMMY COURTNEY

53

Shoveling menhaden from
pound fisherman's boat, Wynne,
Maryland, 1992

*There were any number of people
around Annapolis that, when they
grew up, wouldn't touch a fish or a
crab or an oyster because they had had
to eat it when there was nothing else
to eat. One of the ways to insult a kid
on the playlot, especially those from
Eastport, was to say, "You eat fish,"
denoting that they were so poor that
they couldn't buy real food.*
BERNARD GESSNER

Cat nipping,
Wynne, Maryland, 1992

The problem now is that there's no market-size fish left. If a guy goes out and catches five hundred boxes, they'll only be able to buy a hundred and fifty boxes from him. The rest goes as bait, scrap. He'll get anywhere from a cent and a half to three cents a pound. Not that I'm figuring out all the problems of the Bay, but it's just what's the guy going to do? He's killing himself by catching the small fish, but that little bit of bait money pays his bills.
ANTHONY THOMAS

Cleaning rockfish, Deale, Maryland, 1991

There's too many rockfish. They've eaten the bait up, the blues for one reason or the other have thinned out, and it's taken all the profit away from the commercial fisherman. The state is using the rockfish to get control of the whole industry and the profit margin's going down. The state raised my license fees, meanwhile they took the rockfish away—I need them to make a living right now.

I turned out fifteen thousand pounds of rockfish out there a while ago. That's all I was catching in one particular net. Both my allotments for the year won't be five thousand pounds and I turned out three times that much in one day out of one net. They won't let me catch more than five thousand pounds this year for the whole year. TOMMY COURTNEY

Freighter *Frances* passing beneath the Chesapeake Bay Bridge, 1960

There was a period maybe ten years ago when some folks involved with the port in Hampton Roads really felt that any kind of environmental viewpoint was going to be bad for business for the pilots. I don't hear any of that kind of talk anymore. Most of those guys realize that they can drive those big ships up and down the Bay no matter what the water quality is, but most of them have enough feeling for the Bay to know that it's a lot bigger than just whether they can get ships up and down it or not. JOHN PAGE WILLIAMS

Longshoremen, Baltimore,
Maryland, c. 1962

PREVIOUS SPREAD:
Tug rendezvous, Patapsco River, 1968

Ferry tender James Farington, Whitehaven Ferry,
Wicomico County, Maryland, 1990

*When you go down the river mornings, you can see the moon
still up, and a few minutes later, see the sun coming up, within a
half an hour of each other. And you don't think that's an awe-
some feeling to see that, and hear the waves and the swish of the
seas underneath of the boat? It's like magic.* AUDREY ADAMS

Whitehaven ferry, Wicomico River, 1986

61

Night light, Shady Side, Maryland, c. 1954

I see the watermen as a source of a tremendous amount of information and understanding and an ally in our approach to the Bay. I also see the watermen as independent, sometimes very clever, as egoistic and self-serving as anybody else. In other words, he's trying to do the best for him, with some exceptions. Some have been very generous, very broad-minded, very clever. The waterman knows what he knows better than anybody. Most watermen have worked in one region, and they know every stick and stone on the bottom there. In the old days, they couldn't read a chart, literally couldn't go away from home, but they knew the backyard very well. GENE CRONIN

Crab skiff, Ewell, Maryland, 1965

Most watermen don't really want to retire. You want to just fade away. Even if they retire, they still piddle around with a trotline or something like that. I heard a man say the other day, "What's so good about retiring? What do you do when you retire?" He said he wanted to do something just to kill time. He said, "I don't feel right unless I'm out there."
BOBBY MC KAY

Crabber, Severn River, c. 1960

Land Labor

When we think about the Chesapeake Bay, our imagination immediately turns to being on the water—sailing, oystering, crabbing, fishing—but what we have to realize is that there's a great deal of support and influence that comes from the land that surrounds the Bay. Obviously, the yachts and workboats are built on land, but there are many other activities that make the life of the pleasure boater and the waterman possible.

Over the years I've spent a lot of time in small towns, and there's a different pace of life there. When you get into more rural districts, something as modest as a country store can become the focus for the community. In some of these places, conversation remains an essential form of recreation, and there's a lot of wisdom and tall tales still being swapped around woodstoves. Those situations are getting to be fewer and further between, I'm sorry to say. Convenience stores don't encourage a lot of companionship.

The relationship between farming and the Bay has changed a lot over the years. It used to be that produce grown up the rivers and creeks was loaded onto boats and delivered to markets in Baltimore, Norfolk, and points between; but, of course, now all that is done by truck. Where once a farm on the water meant that you had easy access to water transport, today it usually means that the farmer has a long drive down back roads to get to wholesalers and retail outlets.

What happens on the land has a direct effect on what happens to the Bay, no matter where you are in the watershed. Sometimes I'd get some strange looks when I was talking to someone in the middle of a field and told them that the pictures I was taking were for a book about the Chesapeake Bay, especially when that field was in Pennsylvania or in central Virginia. But that relationship is what I'm trying to convey in my pictures.

Just clearing the land poses an enormous threat to the well-being of the water that adjoins the property. Without trees and their roots and decaying leaves to help keep the soil in place, runoff of soil becomes almost a certainty. The same thing happens when new roads and housing developments are built without effective environmental controls.

I have a lot of sympathy with farmers since I began as a farm boy in Missouri. But at this point in my life, I've spent more years on and near the Bay, and so that's where my concerns are centered now. I've learned that by modifying some of their techniques, farmers can do a lot toward bringing the Bay back to what it used to be.

PREVIOUS SPREAD:
Eastport, Annapolis, Maryland, c. 1960

You'd walk through Eastport and you could always smell the copper from the boats. You know, they had them up, working on them. And you could hear the "clink, clink, clink." It was the sound of summer, I always called it. That was the caulking hammer. Because boats would come open at the seams, the old wooden boats, and quite often they had to caulk them and then put red lead over it and then copper. And that would keep them from leaking for the summer. And some of the men who were looked up to the most were the guys who could really caulk a boat well.
ROGER "PIP" MOYER

Willis Wilson, Deltaville, Virginia, 1993

The watermen are just good-hearted people who just want to make a living the only way they know. Particularly those in their fifties and sixties where there's no turning back now. They want to make a living. They don't want to paint houses. They don't want to supplement their income by doing something that takes away their freedom, their independence. LARRY CHOWNING

Some guys, they leave here full of pride and love for their boat, and if something happens, like it hits something real hard and something happens to it, they'll call me and say, "Oh, I've just busted a piece of my guard. I'd rather for that to have been a chunk took out of my head than would've I done that." You know, that'll tell you right there what they think of their boats. They just don't like to see anything happen to 'em. These guys, they keep their boats up. Some'll kind of let 'em go, but after a while they'll get it refinished and just go again. LARRY MARSH

Marina on Back Creek, Annapolis, Maryland, 1994

Alfred and Downes Curtis,
Oxford, Maryland, 1992

Sail loft, Oxford,
Maryland, 1968

*My sail loft is, I would say, one of the finest erected buildings in town. It's not uneven anywhere.
You can put a chalk line down this floor and it's not an eighth of an inch out. And it's the same
old walls and everything. No paint or nothing has been put up there since I went to school here.*

*I began as a sailmaker working for Dave Pritchett. I guess I was about between eighteen and
twenty. My father sent me over here. I didn't take stock of my age because I didn't want to stay. I
didn't like it. I was getting nine bucks a week. That's the top wages then. My father, he always
said, "Go and stay. What you're learning is worth more than you're getting."*

*They've taken all the art out of sailmaking in the way of hand work, because when I started it
was about seventy-five percent hand and twenty-five percent machine. Now it's about ninety percent machine and only ten percent hand. I bet I know of seven or eight sailmaking firms that all
died off, and the new ones that come along, they're mostly franchised.* DOWNES CURTIS

73

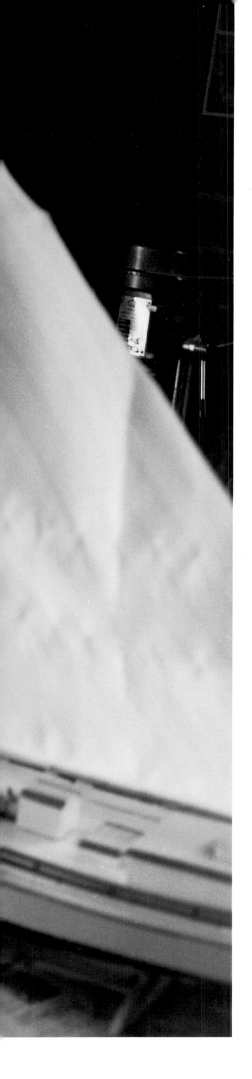

Ewell, Smith Island, Maryland, 1991

Now they have the daily boat, and, of course, the boats that used to take an hour and a half now take forty-five minutes. It's not nearly so bucolic as it was. There was no tourism business really for years, nothing to speak of. There were some tourists, of course, but now there's a business.   REUBEN BECKER

Edward Jones, Ewell, Maryland, 1991

I. P. Hudgins' store, New Point, Virginia, 1993

Back in the thirties, when you lived in Deltaville, if you didn't oyster, you didn't eat. There wasn't nothing else to do around here. Maybe there was one carpenter in Deltaville. Maybe two carpenters. But there wasn't no plumbers because nobody didn't have any indoor toilets; there wasn't no electricians because nobody didn't have no electric; and there weren't no automobile mechanics because nobody didn't have no automobiles. You walked where you was going. Even the storekeepers went oystering in the wintertime. WILLIS WILSON

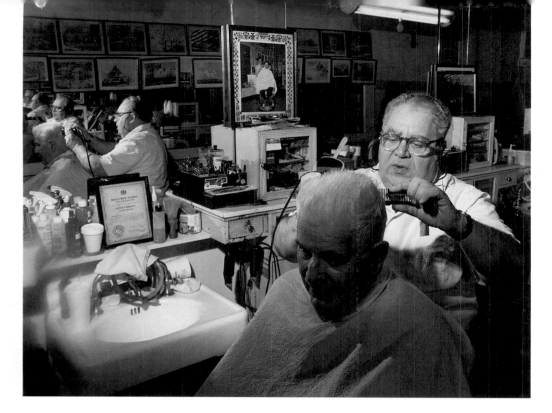

John Calabrese,
Annapolis, Maryland,
1990

Grey's store, Mason Springs,
Maryland, 1990

Detail, tobacco barn near Upper Marlboro, Maryland, c. 1988

When we bought the farm, we had no tractor. We had two mules and two workhorses and two riding horses. The fields were plowed with one man behind a plow. When the crop was put in, it was cultivated, again with one man behind a plow. It was all hand labor.

A tobacco plant is planted in January, February, and the bed is covered over with a cloth. In the first of May, you started transplanting tobacco into the field. Those plants were pulled out of the bed and put on a little trucklike thing that was pulled by a horse, and then fifty million people would get out in the field and start planting the tobacco—every plant. Then you plant twenty-two acres of tobacco, which is nothing. Over in St. Mary's County, they have hundreds of acres of tobacco on one farm.

Tobacco is at least a fifteen-month crop from the time you put it in 'til you sell it. It has to be wormed, and the way to worm it nowadays is not by picking the worms off like they did when we first came here. You spray it. And at one time the county came through and would spray your crop for free.

When it is ready to cut, each stalk of tobacco has to be cut separately and put on a stick, a tobacco stick. Then that is hung in the barns. It can't be hung too close together because it's all air-cured. It is not heat-cured. It hangs there from, say, August until December or January, when it is cured enough to start stripping.

Then each one of those tobacco sticks are taken down, and each leaf is pulled off of the tobacco stalk and patted and fanned out. Then it is put in baskets that are about four-by-four or three-by-three. Then it is ready to pack on the trucks to go to the tobacco warehouses where it is sold.
ETTA W. RICHWINE

Tobacco farm near Bay Ridge,
Anne Arundel County, Maryland, c. 1956

Plowed field in Charles County,
Maryland, 1991

The Europeans quickly learned that the Indians knew where the good land was. The Maryland settlers made a point of finding an Indian village that was about to be deserted long before the soil had been exhausted by the very mild Indian type of agriculture. It took a while to educate Englishmen about where good tobacco land was, how long you could grow corn or tobacco without exhausting the soil, and how to adapt to an Indian agriculture. They had to give up the idea that they could raise English grains and wheat very readily in a place where there was virgin forest.
LOIS GREEN CARR

PREVIOUS SPREAD:
Soybean field, Somerset County,
Maryland, c. 1987

Another thing that is so memorable is the farmers, when they were growing grain, would vie with each other, when they were preparing the fields, for having the finest, levelest field in the area. It never occurred to them that the leveler the field, the finer the grains of soil, the easier it would wash, easier it would blow. The main object was to make it level and smooth so that when it sprouted, it looked beautiful. Well, this was fine if you didn't have heavy rains in the interim, between the time the land was prepared and the time the grains would sprout and grow, but I would say half of the time you'd have a heavy rain or you'd have a windstorm or you'd have something that would take a lot of that topsoil and put it somewhere else where it shouldn't be, and eventually it would wash off into the marsh or the stream or the creek or the river and into the Bay.
WALTER HARRIS

You get a guy farming up here in Surry and you tell him he can't use a certain chemical on his fields because it's going into the Bay, I think they have a hard time stomaching that sometimes. They can't see the relationship where that's going from point A to point B and I guess they don't look at everything in between.

    They've got so many regulations. They've got big jugs of weed killers and they have to be licensed to use the stuff. They have to sit in on a class on how to use it. They have to dispose of it properly. You take a farmer that's been farming, some of these oldtimers, and now all of a sudden they've got to go to a class so that they can buy this stuff that's not as bad as the stuff they bought years ago. DAVE BAUSELL

Contour plowing, Clagett farm,
Prince George's County, Maryland,
1988

Ridge tillage, Clagett farm,
Prince George's County, Maryland,
1987

Loblolly pines near Taylor's Island, Maryland, 1968

When I lived in Baltimore, I didn't know whether it rained or snowed. I didn't care.
I mean, it didn't matter. I went out and got in my car and went to work. Here, it really
matters what the morning is like. It really matters whether it's a cold winter or a mild
winter. REUBEN BECKER

Near Taylor's Island, Maryland, 1968

Sunset near Lancaster, Pennsylvania, 1987

Barn raising, Intercourse, Pennsylvania, 1987

We always had lots of pasture. There were lots of horses on the farm. The manure was spread on the fields where we grew tomatoes. If you put manure on contour-plowed fields, you're not going to have the runoff. Besides that, if you have below the slope a large grassy area, it would be absorbed. WALTER HARRIS

FOLLOWING SPREAD:
Amish farm, Paradise, Pennsylvania, 1987

Migrant workers near Pocomoke, Maryland, 1990

You've got to have a big operation to use migrant labor, particularly now. You have to really provide for the migrant workers a lot better than you used to. Migrant work is the pit of labor, starting with the cane growers in Florida, and they come on up the coast and up through New Jersey, anyway. I don't know how far they go up. I don't see how they get that labor anymore.   ETTA W. RICHWINE

Migrant workers near
Pocomoke, Maryland, 1990

Baling hay, Caroline County,
Maryland, 1988

*I was a farmer's daughter. My father had a big farm, a three-hundred-acre farm. I was one of six
kids. I was the fourth child and the first girl. I never worked in the fields or anything because I had
older brothers that helped my father. I would help my mother. We had chickens, and she'd gather
the eggs or pick the chickens. I never went in the fields at all. That wasn't our job. That was the
boys' job.* MARIAN MC KAY

Courthouse Hill Road, Somerset County, Maryland, 1986

Farmers market, Annapolis,
Maryland, 1990

Selling vegetables, West Point, Virginia, 1990

Produce stand near
Salisbury, Maryland,
1988

The role that women have played has been support, and that support has come in many different ways. They've raised families in the traditional way, not going to work but staying home to make sure that life at home was such that when the men came home it was tolerable. Raising the children to a point where they could go out in the world and be proud of what they are, what they came from, and able to make a living, not letting society have to support them. Women still actually go out and work with their husbands. It's gotten to the point where two heads, three heads, four heads are better than one. In order to survive they've got to get help, and that help often comes from home. LARRY CHOWNING

Women have played such an important part in the development of the Chesapeake Bay region. You don't read much about it in history books, but I firmly believe they have been the backbone of our society. They pointed many of us in the right direction and they do that for watermen. If I didn't have the stability of my home and a wife that supports what I do, I don't know whether I'd be doing what I'm doing, or as happy as I am doing it. I know women have played a tremendous role keeping things together.
LARRY CHOWNING

Cokesbury Road,
Somerset County, 1985

96

Looking Upstream

Few people who live far up the Susquehanna or the Potomac or the James River realize how much the water they're near contributes to the Chesapeake Bay. Oh, they know it flows there eventually, but they don't think about how the waste they throw overboard—or any sewage or industrial contamination—winds up in the Chesapeake Bay. That's why I went up the rivers to photograph them, so that I could carry this message to the people, that upstream has a great influence on the Bay.

It used to be that when we thought about or talked about the Chesapeake, we exalted its immense shoreline and wide vistas, and that's about where it stopped. We thought very little about the impact of the entire watershed. But when we started worrying about the Bay's health, we realized that many of the problems have sources that are far away from the actual tidewater.

You know, it's one thing to stencil the words DON'T DUMP—CHESAPEAKE BAY DRAINAGE on a storm drain in Annapolis, where you can readily understand the relationship, but the greater impact is seeing the same sign on drains in Cumberland or Charlottesville or Cooperstown.

Some of the last picture-taking excursions I made for this book were on the James River in Virginia, including a twelve-hour boat trip to Norfolk. In the lower James, it's easy to relate to the Bay because it's so wide, but above Richmond it narrows considerably and becomes a freshwater, nontidal tributary. You almost forget it has any bearing on the Chesapeake. But when those hilly and mountainous areas flood—which they do fairly often—all kinds of silt and sediment is washed down into the lower James, and eventually some of it empties into the Bay. Around Hopewell, we actually saw a man standing in knee-deep water in the middle of the river just a few yards away from the main shipping channel. It's that shallow.

When we got back at the end of that long day, our skipper said, "You know, I've lived on this river all my life, and you showed me things today that I've never seen before." And that's the whole idea of this book, to show people things they don't see in their own surroundings, let alone the visitor who's never seen the Chesapeake Bay.

Cumberland Narrows,
Allegany County, Maryland,
1958

Georgetown, Maryland,
on the Sassafras River, 1958

The incredible number of miles of
shoreline was always the appeal of the
Chesapeake Bay for me growing up.
The miles of shoreline translated into
all those nooks and crannies, all those
little fingers, more little creeks and
coves and places to anchor than you
could ever explore in a lifetime. That
was the appeal compared to some body
of water that has a fairly straight coast
like San Francisco Bay or the Great
Lakes. There are ports there, but there
aren't all those fingers to disappear
into.

The Chesapeake has an enormous
length of shoreline, so that means you
just go up into a river, and the rivers
branch off into creeks, and the creeks
branch off into other things called
creeks. There aren't enough names for
the hierarchy of fingers that there are.
There's just bay, river, creek, and
that's not enough. There ought to be
about six levels.

Rivers feeding into rivers and creeks
feeding into creeks, and all of them
have these little bumps and holes and
hiding places with deep enough water
for reasonably sized boats to snuggle
into and anchor and just be sur-
rounded by the undeveloped shoreline. That's the appeal for the cruising
sailor. HARVEY WALTERS

101

Allen's Fresh, Maryland, 1992

I do three or four paintings a year of just the marsh—one in the fall, maybe the spring, maybe in late summer—because it's so alive. It's like an organism. The colors change dramatically. In the spring, the greens are so vibrant, there's nothing to describe it—there's no paint—I can use light permanent green and try to add yellow and try all sorts of things to get it up to the right kind of a green, and it's impossible, it's like fluorescent. And the blues and browns. . . . This stuff is hard to explain, but there's things that happen with violets and blues and browns with the plants that are out there. It's indescribable. All you can do is paint it. REUBEN BECKER

I'm not an old man by any means, I'm thirty-five. But I can remember going out in the Bay fishing with my dad when you caught bluefish until you got tired. You caught eight- to ten-pound trout. On a day's trip it was nothing to come home with a full cooler. Now you're lucky if you can find them out there. DAVE BAUSELL

It's sad that you can't look at the water and want to jump into it. As a little girl, when we would go visit friends on the Magothy or the Severn, everybody swam. I don't know of anybody today who swims in the water. So you use it to sail upon or through, but you can't feel the physicalness of it on yourself. I think that's quite tragic. SUZANNE POGELL

Warren's Ferry, Virginia, 1993

Fishing on the Rivanna River,
Columbia, Virginia, 1993

Wenona, Maryland, 1990

Ever since I can remember, I've just loved the water. Whether it be a little creek or a river, I was always fascinated. I always wanted to know what was around the next bend. I've been on every stretch of this river from Richmond to the Bay. You could spend a year out here seeing things that the people that have lived here all their lives never see. You never realize how partial you are to one side of the river until you go the other side and say, "Hey, there's something else over here."
DAVE BAUSELL

A cousin from New England visited me down near Kinsale. We were fishing together, and I said, "We'll go around to the creek." We went around to the creek, and he said, "What's this?" I said, "We're in the creek now." He said, "Hell, this thing's half a mile wide. At home, a creek is something you can jump over." JOHN PAGE WILLIAMS

PREVIOUS SPREAD:
Gray's Creek, near Scotland, Virginia, 1993

Most of the boats you see around here that are sunk are the old round-stern-type boats. They got old. A lot of time people call me up. They think about putting 'em away in the graveyard. They'll call me up and ask me if I want it, to repair it and resell it. But I really don't have the time to do that. I wish I could, because some of these are very old boats, and I would like to restore 'em and see 'em keep going, because when we've lost one, that's one less that I'll have to maintain, and I hate to see 'em get put away.

Put 'em up-a-gut means let 'em just sit there and die. They'll just wore through right away. They'll get worm-eaten, and then they'll begin to rot, and then a little later you look, and she isn't there anymore. She's gone; just the remains of it is all. It's been three or four in the past couple of years that've been put up-a-gut. When your boat's put up-a-gut, she's had it.   LARRY MARSH

Derelict bugeye, Mill Creek, near Solomons, Maryland, 1991

Abandoned skipjack,
Knapps Narrows, Maryland,
1992

Farmers have not learned that if you grow a lot of animals, they make a lot of waste, and it all flows down the creek, and enriches the creek, enriches the river, enriches the Bay. But farmers are extremely hard to change. They are like watermen in that respect. It's hard to convince a farmer on a Pennsylvania milk farm that his cows are hurting somebody fifty miles away, or a hundred miles away, and he should spend money to stop that without any direct benefit to him. So it's a long, slow battle. GENE CRONIN

To some extent, manure's a real resource. You can spread it on land and use it, in many cases, as fertilizer. Used as fertilizer, it saves the farmer his fertilizer bill in the spring. The problem for a lot of those guys is that they've got more manure than they do land, and they've got to do something with it because it continues to pile up. So they start spreading it, and they spread it too thick. They spread it day after day, straight through the year, and they'll do it on a frozen field in the dead of winter. And when they get a heavy rain on that frozen ground, there's no way that stuff's going to work into the soil. It's going to go right off into the river. At its worst, that's a really serious issue. JOHN PAGE WILLIAMS

Amish school house, Intercourse, Pennsylvania, 1987

New Windsor, Carroll County, Maryland, 1992

Susquehanna River
near Towanda, Pennsylvania,
c. 1989

It has been a major specialty of the Chesapeake Bay Foundation all along to provide carefully structured field experience on all kinds of waterways in the Bay watershed. The education program works as far north as Wilkes-Barre and Scranton, Pennsylvania, on the Susquehanna. It works as far west on the west branch of the Susquehanna as Cambria County, which is almost out to Johnstown. It's right on the western edge of the watershed in central Pennsylvania. We have a canoe fleet based in Charlottesville, Virginia, that works all up and down the valley and works out on the edge of the Allegheny plateau. They'll work down as far south as right at the edge of the watershed in Roanoke and all the way up into northern Virginia into Loudoun and Fairfax Counties and right out to the West Virginia line to Lake Moomaw. We work, of course, as far south and east as Hampton Roads, and straight on up the Bay. JOHN PAGE WILLIAMS

Confluence of the James and Rivanna Rivers, Columbia, Virginia, 1993

Richmond is actually built at the fall line, which is where the ships had to stop. That's where Fredericksburg was built on the Rappahanock and Washington was built on the Potomac. They're all built on the fall line, the utmost navigable portion of the river.
PAUL SMITH

Potomac River at Great Falls, Maryland, 1989

The first time I saw the reserve fleet I was about ten or twelve. We were just going down the river from one bend to another and then all of a sudden you see all these things sticking up and it looks like the U. S. Navy is coming at you. The main channel just goes right up through these ships anchored bow to stern.

They're ships in reserve, set up in separate categories as far as the amount of time it would take to get them to a ready status. Some of them are set up to be ready within thirty days, ninety days, up to six months. Some are ready for the scrap yard. They did use some of them in the Persian Gulf crisis. Hopefully they'll sit there idle forever and never have to use them, but I guess they're there if they need them. DAVE BAUSELL

Reserve fleet, James River, 1993

Fishing on the shore of the
Susquehanna River near the
spillway of Conowingo Dam,
1986

Celery was a type of grass that grew in the Bay here. It was good feed for all birds. It is not here anymore. It's been gone since we had that big, big hurricane in 1972. Agnes killed it. Then the government came here and sprayed that whole area to kill some bad growth and they killed everything. That's hard to believe, but they did it.

Conowingo Dam deposited coal dust and sand about two-and-a-half feet deep. That covered everything. They flushed it out. Unbelievable. Things began going down ever since 1927, when they built the dam. They started the dam about '24. R. MADISON MITCHELL

The highest value from a capitalist's point of view is to put a house on waterfront property. But then you have one family that gets to use the river at that point as opposed to opening it up to the public for the people who don't live on the water. It's not cost effective to build a marina anymore. Between the land costs and the engineering costs, to develop on the water has become just phenomenal. It's very difficult for a marine contractor to find enough work in this atmosphere of protectionism for the environment. There's got to be a better balance than we've currently got. PAUL SMITH

Jug Bay, Prince George's County, Maryland, 1986

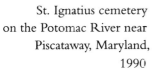

St. Ignatius cemetery on the Potomac River near Piscataway, Maryland, 1990

Home Ports

I like to travel country roads. You don't see much from main roads, but if you go down little country roads, you can come across all kinds of interesting things, so whenever possible, I take a shortcut—not a shortcut, a long cut—to wherever I'm going. Sometimes I just look at the map and try to find the most remote destination I can—that's how I discovered Elliott and Saxis and Bavon.

Much of the enjoyment of this project has come from following a road to its end. There's so much to see and do along the way, and the beauty of it is, it's a very inexpensive way to spend the day. The restaurants in some of these small communities, particularly when they're by the water, serve some of the best seafood around. I enjoy a fancy meal as much as anyone, but it's pretty hard to beat a crabcake made from crabmeat that was picked that morning.

Sampling the bounty by the roadside is also rewarding. I think that today a lot of people are shy about going to church suppers or community oyster roasts where they feel they don't belong, but nothing could be further from the truth. I've found that local people are very welcoming to strangers who patronize their activities, they're very proud of what they're offering. And it's such fine eating! It's all home-cooked, the portions are usually big, and the price is always very reasonable.

Deciding what kinds of activities I wanted to portray in my Bay Project was easy. I figured the departments of tourism and the chambers of commerce do a great job of promoting the obvious attractions of the Chesapeake region, the kinds of things the average sightseer encounters. I wanted to show what it's like to live here every day, the kinds of things you have to get off the beaten track to see.

Of course, Smith Island is the definition of remote since you have to take a twelve-mile boat ride to get there. It was tempting to spend too much time there because it seemed to embody everything I like best about the Chesapeake Bay region: the people are warm and friendly, the boats are plentiful and well kept, and the marsh is teeming with wildlife and texture. Everywhere I looked there were fascinating subjects for my camera.

I never tire of searching out new vantage points along the Bay, whether I'm on new territory or exploring the familiar twists and turns along the Severn River. After all my explorations, though, it's always good to return to my own home port, Annapolis.

City Dock,
Annapolis, Maryland, c. 1963

Morning boat from Smith Island to Crisfield, Maryland, 1992

When I came to Smith Island, I had this really—I thought at the time—brilliant observation that this was a microcosm and I was going to learn more about the world and people, living on this little island, than I would in Baltimore. I've not been disappointed in that at all, because I think I have. In the twenty years I've been here, I've become so aware of how people interact, and I've had really dear friends die all around me and be born. You live on the mainland, and if you don't like a group of people, you can move away from them. Or if you don't like that person, you just don't see him. It's impossible here. If you hate somebody, you see him every day.

People do, in a small group, play out all the things that the whole world does. Then if you extend that idea, the Bay is a microcosm for the world, and the exercises we go through here to save the Bay are very close, in the end, to what we're going to do to save the world or not. And that's really the way I look at it.

So the future is just as good here as anywhere, and just as bad here as anywhere. As far as this little island is concerned, I think it will probably be here quite a while yet. Maybe in slightly changed form, but I think it'll be here a while. REUBEN BECKER

PREVIOUS SPREAD:
Sunrise on Spa Creek, Annapolis, Maryland, 1993

On the hot hazy mornings it's really a joy to see how the sun is going to emerge. In August, it's a bright red ball. On those kinds of days the sea actually looks like molten lead. I've never seen a sea look like the Chesapeake does when it's hot. It's grey with a sheen to it. SUZANNE POGELL

Ewell, Smith Island, Maryland, 1967

Marsh at Ewell,
Maryland, 1992

*The island itself is very protected. We're in this little pocket around the back of the Eastern Shore.
The worst I've ever seen was Hurricane Gloria. We had sixty-, seventy-five-mile-an-hour winds,
but that was about it. A lot of people leave. I don't think they used to, but I think they do now.
I've never left anytime. I'm too interested to see what will happen. But a lot of people go to
Crisfield. Many people over here have relatives all over the Eastern Shore. This was like the cradle
of the Eastern Shore.* REUBEN BECKER

Tylerton is the best place in the world to raise children. Anybody going to have a family, they ought to move to Tylerton to do it. Your neighbors are so close. There are no fences; the kids are just in one yard, then they're wandering in another. They grow up learning to respect the water. Now, some child could go out and drown this afternoon, you know, but it's not happened in my lifetime. They're taught that from an early age, to be careful if you go on wharves. JANICE MARSHALL

Elliott, Maryland, 1986

Smith Island,
Maryland, 1965

123

Cokesbury Road near Pocomoke,
Maryland, 1991

Virginia Route 695 near Saxis,
Virginia, 1989

Home port, Elliott, Maryland, 1986

You see a bad storm come up sometime, and, man, you see 'em moving their boats. It looks like they say, "Well, I'll tend to the house later. I've got to get my boat to safety." That boat's their pride and joy. That's what they make their living in, and they take care of it. It's the best thing they've ever had, really, because some boys around here owns these boats, and they're afraid to even have a scratch on it, but they know it's gonna be put there on account of what they do in it. They take care of it like somebody would their car over on the mainland. LARRY MARSH

Nassawadox, Virginia, 1989

It's a one-street town. On one side of the street is the railroad and the other side of the street are the stores. There was a couple restaurants in there when I was there, and a hardware store, ice plant, maybe one or two women's stores, and some residences. The railroad is still there, and I think it's still working.   WILLIS WILSON

The men would go in the afternoon to the store, and they'd all sit around a potbellied woodstove and talk about how many oysters they caught yesterday and where they were going tomorrow and "What do you think the weather's going to be?" The biggest topic was the weather, whether you were going to be able to get out on the water or not. A lot of times they would play cards. There was no gambling there. It was just like 58 or rummy.

Women didn't go and sit in no store. That was a man's place. You went in and got your groceries and got out as fast as you could. I wasn't interested in what the weather was. I was more interested in just going home and cooking and getting the kids ready for school the next day.
AUDREY ADAMS

PREVIOUS SPREAD:
Arundel on the Bay, Fishing Creek,
and Thomas Point, Maryland, 1970

St. Michaels, Maryland, 1986

Sailing on Chesapeake Bay brings back history. You feel as if you're in an age-old environment. For so many of us, looking at something that isn't changing much too fast is pleasurable. I guess that's why everybody likes to go to Eastern Bay, to St. Michaels, and Oxford, and Cambridge, because it feels as though it's been there a long time and the scale of it is very human. The connection with the Bay is very close. SUZANNE POGELL

Card players, Bloxom, Virginia, 1989

Grandparents' day at school,
Tylerton, Maryland, 1991

Schoolhouse, Warsaw, Virginia, 1986

The school will probably close if it's not enough children. We've got a baby on Tylerton now that's not quite a year old, but the father's just waiting to find a job on the mainland so that he can move. My daughter's getting ready to have another baby. That'll be another baby. What's two babies? I believe as long as it's two or three kids in school, they'll keep it open, because it's a problem transporting small children across water. JANICE MARSHALL

Camp meeting, Smith Island,
Maryland, 1991

Camp meeting is like a big homecoming, really. We have an evangelist come in for a week, and we have famous gospel groups come in and help with the services. It's something you look forward to all year.

We have one service in the morning and one in the afternoon and one at night. It's a real special time, and we hope and pray that another soul is saved and there'll be seeds planted. Spiritual seed what will cause that little gnawing deep down inside that you know you need a different way of life. Life's hard now, and you need that something special to help get you through it. Half times you don't see it, but you need that special feeling and that spiritual high. It's not like a drug high or alcohol high, but that high that comes from the heart. BRENDA HARRISON MARSH

There's not too much at all for young people to do here now. They go off. Years ago, Saturday night, there would be cars running up and down the road and parties along the road. That happens rarely now. There just aren't enough.

When I think of it, over the past couple of years, I can only think of about two weddings here. Now there are more funerals than weddings. Funerals outnumber the weddings five to one. Ten to one.

I think the signs are the island is dying. If for no other reason just attrition. In the time that I've been here many of the old standard Smith Islanders are gone. Some of my best friends—I've really enjoyed some of these people that I've met—and they're just gone. And there's nobody to replace them as the children leave. There's a certain number that have stayed. There's some young watermen around, too, but the business is shrinking. REUBEN BECKER

Carnival at North Beach,
Maryland, 1985

*One to two children is it for most peo-
ple now. It's hard to support a family.
A lot of girls marry away. Some of
them stay and marry watermen. The
boys wants to stay here, and the girls
wants to leave. So there's the problem.
Now, my son, I never encouraged him
to be on the water, never, because it's
too hard. You make money, but by the
time you save a little bit of money, it's
time to put it back in your rig.*
JANICE MARSHALL

Hanging out on Smith Island, Maryland, 1991

St. James African Methodist
Episcopal Church,
Oriole, Maryland, 1991

*This no Sunday crabbing, you say religion makes us do that. They figured out your body needs a
day of rest. I'll tell you what happens when you work Sundays. Next week, you're going to lose
one of those days, and either you or your engine's not going to stand it, and you're going to lose a
day somewhere along there, so we take it off voluntarily, hoping to rest both man and the engine.*

*We've been doing it for hundreds of years. I don't know of anybody hungry or homeless here.
If it is, I don't know who they are. We're not rich, but we're not laying under a newspaper either.
So what the heck more do you want if you can feed your family?*   JENNINGS EVANS

*The majority of people goes to church. They realize where their livelihood comes from. When
you're a waterman, you don't go out and you don't plant seeds, or you don't do anything in the
way of preparation of your harvest. There's got to be Somebody there that provides that.*
BRENDA HARRISON MARSH

St. Elizabeth's Roman
Catholic Church,
Westover, Maryland,
1986

First Baptist Church,
near Mathews, Virginia,
1993

If you went into Rock Hall, the boats that you see berthed there, used for oystering, crabbing, and pound netting and gill netting, they'd be different than the boats you'd see in Crisfield. Down in the lower Bay, in certain parts, they say that the boat has to be forty feet long or else it won't fit the sea. The crests of the waves are farther apart than they are up here, and your waterman feels it when he's out every day. He knows what type of boat fits the water that he's working on most comfortably. A boat that's suitable in the Chester River may be very narrow, because it's an efficient hull to move through the water under power and it's suitable for oyster tonging and it also can fit into a more narrow slip, which costs less money to rent. But if you take it to the lower Bay, it's going to roll too much or it's going to ship water. It just won't be suitable for the weather conditions that prevail. FRED HECKLINGER

Knapps Narrows,
Tilghman Island, Maryland,
1987

The engineering cost on a residential pier can be excessive. Fortunately, for a residential open-pile pier, the process is not so encumbered that you usually can get that fairly easily. If you want to do anything past that, whether it's a bulkhead, a boat ramp, dredging—either residential or commercial—it's a long process. You can spend anywhere from three months to never to get your permits. The agencies seem to thrive on justifying their position more so than getting the job done.
PAUL SMITH

Skiffs, Shady Side, Maryland, 1985

Wetlands anchorage near Deal Island, Maryland, c. 1951

There really is a thing about the water, and it's one of the reasons I'm here. I'm working on a painting right now that is nothing but the end of my yard and the beginning of the marsh, because to me, that's life. I mean, that's reality. The marsh is where it all started and where ultimately it will all end. And it's that closeness to the water, and particularly the marsh, particularly this water, particularly the Bay water. I feel more intrigued by the marsh than I do by the surf. To go to the ocean, that's all very nice and pretty, but boy, this is complicated here. REUBEN BECKER

Any locality in the world tends to develop boats suitable for the type of work that they do. The log canoe in Central America is going to be a slightly different shape than it is in the Congo. In the Chesapeake Bay, one of the conditions is the vessel has to be a very shallow draft. They have to be able to go into shallow water because the harbors are usually shallow.

The boats built in Deltaville, that are used in the lower Bay around the York River, Mobjack Bay, and the Rappahannock River, have much more flare forward. The water down there is choppier and it keeps the spray from coming on board. A vessel that's berthed out of Kent Narrows, that is only going to go to oyster tonging in Eastern Bay or the Chester River, is an entirely different type of boat. Although it's a power boat that has a single engine and is pointed on one end and blunt on the other, it's a rather different design. FRED HECKLINGER

Upside down, Tylerton,
Maryland, 1991

Bavon, Virginia, 1993

I imagine it's forty, fifty clammers on the Bay now. They would go oystering if they had any oysters to catch. You take that clamming, they have to go out in the middle of the Bay, and it's so rough out there. Well, if the wind is ten or fifteen miles, you can't work out there for clamming. But you can work in the river here patent tonging in twenty-five, thirty.   WILLIS WILSON

I'll say thirty percent of the watermen around here have a summertime boat and a wintertime boat. By the time they have maintenance work done on both of 'em like a couple of times a year, that's pretty expensive. They go patent tonging in the winter to catch oysters. And in the summer they crab-scrape.   LARRY MARSH

Clam rigs, Broad Creek,
Deltaville, Virginia, 1993

You end up with a heavily industrialized waterfront, and the result in both Hampton Roads and in Baltimore is that you lose a fair amount of habitat with bulkheaded shorelines, with urban run-off. Now, that doesn't mean necessarily that those waterways ought to be given up on. It does mean that we maybe lower our expectations a little bit. You don't expect to find the same kind of habitat in the Patapsco or the Elizabeth River that you would find up in the Chickahominy or up at the head of the Nanticoke. JOHN PAGE WILLIAMS

Baltimore & Ohio Railroad piers at Locust Point, Baltimore, Maryland, c. 1960

Inner Harbor, Baltimore, Maryland, 1984

143

Sunrise on the Wye River at Bennett Point, Maryland, c. 1988

I think the contrasts are what is fascinating. You can come around a turn and you're in a quiet, secluded bay where you still feel that there's a lot of natural life that isn't disturbed. The disturbing thing is when you see how filthy the water is. Environmentally we have been very unkind to our waters. We're not treating them any better now than we did before, even with all the concentration of money and concern. We're still dumping stuff and causing the water to be so opaque that nothing can grow down there. SUZANNE POGELL

Aircraft carriers *John F. Kennedy* and *America*
berthed at Norfolk, Virginia, 1993

Causes and Cures

When I started my Bay Project, people asked me what it was going to be about and my answer was always, "I don't know." People thought I was crazy. If I was going to do a book, how could I not know what it was about? It was a mind-fix of mine not to know, so that I would not be tempted to prejudge what I was going to find.

I took lots of pictures of obvious concerns like erosion and pollution, but many problems are impossible to photograph. How do you show subaquatic vegetation that isn't there? How do you show the dermo and MSX that are wiping out the oysters? So I began making pictures that I felt symbolized the sources of the problems that threaten the Bay.

Even before I started, I knew that my subject was controversial. I knew that there was disagreement among watermen, environmentalists, politicians, developers, and farmers about what the challenges were and not much consensus about how to solve them. I knew that I was no expert, but I cared a lot about this place I call home, and I thought that I could help to concentrate the attention of the public by illustrating the issues in a compelling way. As *I* learned more about the Bay, so would the entire community.

Overcrowding is one factor that everyone agrees is a serious problem. Campaigns begun a generation ago to attract tourists to the area were too successful. Many visitors decided that the Chesapeake Bay is not only a desirable place to vacation, it's also a very attractive area to live in. Communities from Baltimore to Bozman offer tremendous opportunities for those who enjoy being near the water. The beaches are pleasant, and the scenery at the end of just about any road that borders the Bay or its tributaries is often breathtaking.

So many visitors moving here because they like the quality of life means more boats dumping oil and sewage, more roads, more clearing of land, more waste to treat, and more shopping centers with their vast parking lots. All of these elements combine to threaten the Bay's well-being.

This population explosion is layered on top of the pollution caused by long-established industries and the challenges posed by natural diseases like dermo and MSX. Is it any wonder that when I started this project, people were talking about the impending death of the Chesapeake Bay?

Hackett Point,
Anne Arundel County,
Maryland, 1986

147

Oil in grasses,
Powhatan Creek,
Jamestown, Virginia,
1993

Everything that's wrong with the Chesapeake Bay added up, I think, to the state that it's in now, economically for the fisherman and environmentally for the Bay. A waterman, he puts oil in his boat, overboard goes the container. His bilge gets full of oil, he looks around, and overboard it goes. They're their own worst enemy. You have twice as many boats, twice as much oil, killing twice as many fish, half as much are left to catch. So what do you do? ANTHONY THOMAS

I get no joy at all out of the water around here now. To me it's like riding the subway. It's so crowded. And you can't swim. You'd be afraid to swim. There's no fish up this way. And about the only thing you can do is, maybe, a little bit of crabbing now, and that's even tough because you're in each other's way with all the ninety-mile-an-hour boats out there—the big power boats. It's like riding the subway. ROGER "PIP" MOYER

Back Creek, Annapolis,
Maryland, 1985

I am convinced that just the sheer numbers of people will reach a level some day that there will be a point of no return for the Chesapeake Bay. The Bay is a shallow body of water; so are the rivers. We can't tolerate the addition of millions and millions of people that want to live in the Chesapeake Bay basin and clean the Chesapeake Bay up. I think it's sheer folly to expect both to happen. The planners will say if we plan properly and have good land use, we can have all the people in the world here. That just isn't so. BERNIE FOWLER

Fishing on the
Susquehanna Flats, 1963

149

James River at Richmond, Virginia, 1993

Up around Richmond, usually when you get the worst flooding is when the rain comes out of the mountains. We could have flood conditions in Richmond and never really have had any rain. I remember going up to Drewry's Bluff below Richmond and seeing cattle carcasses floating down the river, rooftops floating down the river. Right now to this day there's an old bus on the bank. You're just going along the river and all of a sudden there's this city bus right there on the riverbank.

    Now Richmond is building this floodwall with millions of dollars to protect these businesses from flooding. Ain't a whole lot of stuff man can build that's going to control Mother Nature. I think the more you build, and the more you try to control, the more she's going to show you that she's going to have the upper hand. DAVE BAUSELL

Warren's Ferry, Virginia, 1993

The erosion is from west of Richmond, coming out of the foothills. It floods regularly. When you say "flood" it's not what they have on the Mississippi, but if you just get four or five inches of rain over a weekend west of Richmond, two or three days later we have the waters near flood stage or slightly over. It comes down the river at a real high velocity and carries the silt with it.
PAUL SMITH

Anne Arundel County, Maryland, 1992

Growing houses instead of farms is a problem not just, say, in Harford County or Howard County or Anne Arundel County, but also in places like Lancaster County, Pennsylvania, where the eastern part of the county is becoming outer-ring suburbs for Philadelphia.

Land-use issues range from residential housing and office park development to agriculture. The solutions are going to lie somewhere between voluntary programs with good incentives and regulatory programs. It's going to take some regulation to push people into the voluntary programs. Voluntary programs, especially the agricultural programs in Pennsylvania, Maryland, and Virginia, have all picked up farmers over the years, but invariably it's numbers like ten and fifteen percent of the state's farms instead of larger numbers.
JOHN PAGE WILLIAMS

Power, Anne Arundel County, Maryland, 1985

I always said that a developer, he'd build something on top of his mama's grave if he thought he could make a dollar off of it. Everywhere you see something pretty and they bring in the bulldozers and clear it off and put something up and sell it or rent it out. The more people there are, the more people need recreation, the more people go to the river. So I guess there's more need for houses and condominiums, but where do you stop it? Where do you draw the line? DAVE BAUSELL

The Downs on the Severn River, 1991

153

Turbines at Conowingo Dam, Conowingo,
Maryland, 1986

*People say, "I don't really like this industrial plant built on the
river bank." Well, that's fine, we can tear the plant down, but
you're not going to be able to buy any more carpet. Same thing with
these ships that run aground and tear a hole in the bottom and leak
oil. People get all upset, but at the same time, park your car and
start walking. It's that simple. There's a balance out there, for sure,
between safety, economics, environment. Probably you'd say the
American people are wasteful, but you can't just stop what we're
doing and go back to coonskin caps and log cabins. Society won't
allow that either.* PAUL SMITH

Three Mile Island nuclear power plant,
Pennsylvania, 1988

154

Erosion on the
Choptank River, 1986

I would guesstimate that the banks have moved back in excess of a hundred feet on each side over fifteen or sixteen years through one particular area. The banks just wash back and cave in. They're moving back steadily. The river's going to do what it wants to do. It has more power than man can ever control.
PAUL SMITH

Waterskiing on Back River near
Jamestown, Virginia, 1993

We're all to blame for the Bay's present condition. It didn't just occur overnight; it's been something that's been going on for centuries.

A lot of people don't think about this, because they are just so intent on enjoying life and enjoying the river and the Bay with their motorboats. Outboards, particularly, cause a lot of damage because their props stir up the creeks, and many times they drag the keel or the outboard into the grass. They're stirring up the sediment, and I think this has a lot to do with the grasses not growing. It keeps the shallow areas stirred up because the sediment from the fields is down in the bottom of the creek. It's caused by improper farming done decades ago. WALTER HARRIS

People think that if you can throw it in the river and wait for it to go around the corner, then it isn't your problem anymore. There are people who are upriver and people who are downriver, and they have different points of view. Hence, the nice little prayer about "Do unto others downstream as you would have others upstream do unto you." And how do you get people to realize that just by throwing it in the river and waiting until it goes around the corner doesn't solve the problem in general, although it might solve yours? ROCKWOOD FOSTER

Blackwalnut Point,
Tilghman Island, Maryland,
1989

FOLLOWING SPREAD:
Erosion at Elliott's Island, Maryland, 1993

157

Debris from clear-cutting timber
on the road from Crisfield to Pocomoke,
Maryland, 1989

*Cutting down trees along streams tends to heat them up at the same time that they get loaded up
with sediment. What that works toward is warm murky water with mucky bottoms instead of
cooler, clearer, gravel bottoms, which are natural habitats for most of the creatures in those streams.*
JOHN PAGE WILLIAMS

Lumber mill near Goochland, Virginia, 1993

*When you look at different areas of the Bay and you see decline, particularly in the oyster industry,
you can point, if you go back historically, to different reasons for it. It may have been a hurricane.
It may have been a pulp mill. A lot of times it goes back to the beginning of this country. In the
very beginning when they started putting gristmills on ponds, the local governments and local
authorities turned their heads away from the Chesapeake Bay water and looked to what they
thought was more important: the development of land on the Chesapeake Bay and the development of land in this country.* LARRY CHOWNING

Hopewell, Virginia, 1993

Back when I was growing up, the old school cheer was "I smell, you smell, we all smell Hopewell." Back then they were proud of Hopewell. When you came into town on the main road there was a big sign: Welcome to Hopewell, Chemical Capital of the South. After the Kepone incident, the signs started coming down.

They started having some fish kills, and some people that worked in the plant started suffering from these nervous disorders, and come to find out this Kepone was major bad stuff. I don't think anybody knew the extent of it until they started probing around. The river was shut down. To this

day, when you get brochures from the state of Virginia about the fishing regulations, there's an advisory on there for the James River.

They shut the river down from Richmond to Newport News. There were lawsuits left and right. That adversely affected everybody from the recreational fisherman wanting to go out to catch supper to these commercial fishermen. All of a sudden, you're fishing one day and the next day you can't. What do you do? Move?   DAVE BAUSELL

Dairy farm near Olney, Maryland, 1986

What you end up with are sewage problems if they've really got animals packed on relatively small pieces of land. A single dairy cow puts out a hundred pounds of manure a day, and you go 365 days with a two-hundred-cow herd, that's a lot of manure. The working number that we toss around, which is at least reasonably correct: Lancaster County has got four hundred thousand people in it, but sewage and manure combined, it puts out the sewage equivalent of a city of five million. JOHN PAGE WILLIAMS

Charlie's chickens, Somerset County, Maryland, 1990

Areas like the Eastern Shore of Maryland, in the Shenandoah Valley of Virginia, and in central Pennsylvania, especially York, Lancaster, Lebanon Counties, there are farmers doing a lot of intensive animal husbandry. Now, you look at the variety of it, and you might look at things like turkeys in Augusta County, Virginia, down around Staunton. Obviously, on the Eastern Shore of Maryland, it's chickens. In central Pennsylvania, it might be dairy cattle.

The Shore is beginning to have to worry about it because chicken manure is very concentrated, especially in nitrogen. They've got sandy soils, and both they and the folks in Lancaster County are running the risk of polluting the groundwater with nitrogen. They've got substantial percentages of wells that have got nitrogen contamination. JOHN PAGE WILLIAMS

164

No-till farming near Easton,
Maryland, 1986

No-till system requires leaving every bit of organic material that you can from the crops on the fields, building up a layer of mulch that absorbs the water when the rains occur. The ground is shaded; the ground stays more moist. There is never a drought with the system because you have a mulch covering the entire area.

A lot of people find that their problems with bugs increase. If you see a problem developing, you may have to use some herbicide. But you don't do this until you actually see the problem has reached a point where it's going to be devastating. The stuff is very expensive, and you don't want to use it unless you have to.   WALTER HARRIS

Farmers checking the gauge at a water station, Warsaw, Virginia, 1991

We've tightened up our use of poisonous chemicals on farms a great deal. In fact, we're making the farmers pay a good bit of the cost, but not all of it. And farmers have learned that we're serious about keeping sediment on the ground and they want that. They don't want to lose their sediment.
GENE CRONIN

The Anacostia is an important tributary of Chesapeake Bay. They found and identified all the streams in the District of Columbia that feed into the Anacostia and have gotten the people who live nearby all excited about clearing up, let's say, Watts Branch, which is the big one. The children are studying this in school, and the science classes are taking samples of Watts Branch and testing it as part of their science projects, and they're collecting what little fish are still in there and seeing if they're growing bigger year to year, which they are.

We have found that you can get people initially much more interested in their own stream that goes right by their backyard than thinking about the Chesapeake, which is far away. When you get interested in Watts Branch, then you say, "Well, where does Watts Branch go?" Eventually intelligent people will ask that, and they'll say, "Oh, into the Anacostia." And then eventually they learn the Anacostia goes to the Potomac, and the Potomac goes to Chesapeake Bay. This process of moving the Chesapeake Bay program back into the tributaries is under way now in all states that affect the Chesapeake Bay. ROCKWOOD FOSTER

Anacostia neighborhood clean-up project, Bladensburg, Maryland, 1990

The Chesapeake Bay Foundation's educational program was Arthur Sherwood's idea originally. Arthur had this nice, simple idea that the best way to teach people about the Bay was to take them out on it, and that's been the foundation of everything we've done since then. Everything we do is grounded in firsthand field experience on the Bay. We've put well over a quarter million people through the program over the last twenty years.

We structure the program so that no matter how much experience somebody's got with the Bay, we can take them deeper. Watermen's kids from the Northern Neck, say, who got a lot of field experience on their own, fishing with their parents and grandparents, we try to help them see some things from new points of view. Very often they'll find that they get insights into questions that have been rattling around in their heads for five years.

At the same time, we take inner-city kids from D.C. and Baltimore who have never been out on a boat before, and we have to work in a very basic sense with them. We try to reach people where they are, simple as that. We encourage them to learn their own home waterways, like Baltimore Harbor, like the Potomac in Washington, like the Bay in Annapolis, or like the Elizabeth River in Norfolk. At the same time, we encourage them to look at parts of the Bay that are different from where they've been, too. JOHN PAGE WILLIAMS

Chesapeake Bay Foundation educational cruise, Rhode River, 1986

Tom Wisner and Mary Sue Kaelin, 1987

169

I see the Bay as a continuing political focus. I go back to the days when the watermen used to storm in in their gumboots and demand things of the legislature and scare them to death, and they got what they wanted. Even though they were only a small number of the total picture, they were so vocal and so frightening that nobody on the Eastern Shore would vote against the watermen's wishes. That's changed. It's changed with representation. Maryland used to have thirteen senators on the Eastern Shore and now we have three. So the waterman doesn't have the clout he did.
GENE CRONIN

Dermo has moved upstream, and maybe we carried it up there with the seed oysters. Dermo gets in the oysters and will not leave. Now, it's going to be interesting to see whether all of this runoff is going to drive it out. If it does, maybe we have a chance in a couple of years to get back in it. The other problem is, are we at such a low ebb that the seed oysters won't be regenerated? If they won't, then we're done for. SKIPPER GARRETT

Planting oyster shells,
James River, 1993

Governors Harry Hughes and Charles Robb
inspecting an oyster bed near Irvington, Virginia,
1985

*We invited Governor Harry Hughes to travel down the Patuxent
River with us in December 1979. We actually dredged the oysters
up in the northern reaches of the river and they shucked the oysters
and he watched the oysters die. He watched it shrink up to nothing
right before his eyes. They also showed him records on the transparency of the river. The governor was convinced, and he said it was
time that we went to work.*   BERNIE FOWLER

*The question on environment has to do with the disposal of waste of all kinds, whether you're talk-
ing about sanitary waste, whether you're talking about storm sewers, whether you're talking about
trash. There are only three places to throw things away. You can either put it in the air by burning
it, you can put it in the water by dumping it in the river, or you can bury it in the land. That's the
only three choices you've got.*

*The politics of it are that you've got clean-air people, you've got clean-water people, and you've
got clean-land people. Your clean-air people say, "Don't mess up the air which we breathe. Put it
in the water or in the land." But if you're a water person, you say, "Oh, no, don't put it in the
water. Either bury it or incinerate it." And you can see that around a table where you have people
who are extremists, you always get two against one. Nothing ever really gets solved. It is extremely
difficult for legislators to deal with this because they get bombarded by these three groups.*
ROCKWOOD FOSTER

Wetlands development protest,
Back Bay, near Shady Side,
Maryland, 1992

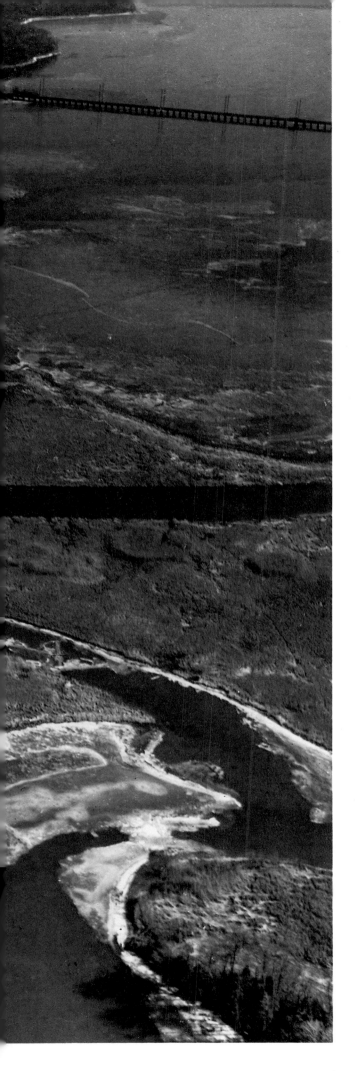

Osprey, Assateague, Virginia, 1969

Ospreys have come back a long way. It's pretty well documented that they've come back in the last few years in the upper rivers and in the lower rivers as well. You go out and poke around in the Severn, and the ospreys are beginning to build nests on a lot of the channel markers.

These birds have a pretty tight window of needs for growth because they're born in late May or early June. They have to be fledged by late July so that they can spend August learning to fish, so that by early September they can pull out of here and head for their other summer in Central and South America. Some of these birds that are hatched every year on the Bay are as far down as Argentina by October, which by any measure is a staggering achievement. JOHN PACE WILLIAMS

Willy Warner keeps in touch with the Smith Islanders he wrote about in Beautiful Swimmers. *He calls them up every year and says, "How are things?" He called this fellow down in Tylerton on Smith Island, and the man said, "Well, Mr. Warner, they're getting a little better. The grasses are starting to come back." He says, "You know, Mr. Warner, God's gonna bring the grasses back and the politicians are gonna take the credit for it."* GENE CRONIN

Middle River, 1985

Pleasant Living

Descriptions of the Chesapeake Bay as a land of pleasant living go back to the earliest colonial days. Living near the crabs, fish, oysters, and clams—to be eaten fresh, right out of the Bay—has always been appreciated by the people who live here. Our climate is varied. We have four very distinct seasons, but it rarely gets below zero and our hot spells really don't last that long. With the breezes off the water, it's pretty tolerable. The humidity is high, but no place is perfect.

Even wildlife find the Bay a pleasant place to live. Whether you travel by land or by water, if you look around, you're likely to see thousands of geese, ospreys, swans, herons, and even some eagles. I like to hunt them out with my camera, but there are lots of folks who consider this area a prime place for gunning.

In Annapolis we have thousands of visitors every year who come to see the old buildings, and while they're here, some of them discover the Bay almost by chance. History is all around us in the Chesapeake Bay region. Many of the handsome Georgian homes have survived, and archaeologists are finding all sorts of evidence from the colonial period, as well as traces of the Indian cultures who were here long before the European settlers arrived.

People who grew up here seem to enjoy different attributes of the region than the often more affluent newcomers. Natives out for a day of fishing are just as likely to drop their lines from a workboat as a modern motorboat. Recent arrivals crowd into Kentucky Fried Chicken, while local folks socialize at chicken barbecues sponsored by local churches or the Kiwanis. And well before the tradition of enormous boat shows was established in Annapolis, people knew that the ideal place to see the best and the newest in technology was at county fairs.

Documenting people in their natural environment is what I've tried to emphasize in these photographs. When I come upon a group of people with my camera, they usually change their position and become self-conscious. I just watch and wait until they lose interest in me. One of my tricks is to set the camera on a tripod, focus on them, and walk away from it. They usually go back to what they were doing, and after a while I quietly but quickly step back to the camera and push the shutter. That spontaneity is what I value most in a photograph.

Harbor at St. Michaels,
Maryland, 1986

I see the Bay changing from the great seafood center it was to principally recreational and transportation uses. You can still go sailing even though there are no fish down there. You can still take a power boat and go where you want in the Bay. You can still live along the water and play on the beach and look at the water, and most of it doesn't look changed.

GENE CRONIN

I remember in the early fifties, when I first started sailing, I was in an old eight-meter boat. It was based out of Oxford. Sherman Hoyt and I would sail up here on a Friday for the weekend races off Annapolis. If, on a Friday, you saw another boat under way, it was something to talk about, and you usually knew who it was. On some of the weekends, there may have been so many boats you might have been confused some of the time, but there still were not many.

FRED HECKLINGER

Yacht race, Chesapeake Bay, c. 1953

Sailing, you can almost pretend that none of the problems exist. There you are, out there on the water in harmony with Mother Nature, or challenging Mother Nature. With the wind blowing, with the sea sparkling, the spume of the sea coming up in front of you in the spray, you really feel as if you're totally away from the workaday world and doing something for yourself.

That's the exciting thing about sailing. It's the opportunity to recreate oneself, to be fully in command of what's going on. You have immediate gratification for your labors: you pull something and something happens; you trim the sail and the boat goes faster. And all of this is at the pace of five or six nautical miles an hour, but it feels so much better than going ninety-five miles an hour in a car. SUZANNE POGELL

Yachts near
Annapolis, Maryland,
c. 1958

A cruising sailor might be interested in making their boat go, but they're more interested in the overall experience of being on the water, getting somewhere, dropping anchor, enjoying the surroundings and life on board the boat. The competitive sailor is only there for the race. They care about making the boat go fast and care about winning. They might love sailing and love being on the water, but once the race is over, they might not care at all. They'd be happy to be airlifted back ashore. They're not interested in a leisurely sail back home. That's not true for everyone, but I think most people fall into one or the other category. HARVEY WALTERS

Racing aboard *Freedom*, Chesapeake Bay, c. 1955

Ed Cutts says if God intended you to have a fiberglass boat he'd build a fiberglass tree.   DOWNES CURTIS

There's boats here, and not only boats here, but boats other places around here, that the people ain't seen them for two years, the owners. They just keep paying slip rental onto them and ain't even seen them. Now, back about in the thirties, there weren't but about seven or eight boats on this creek.
WILLIS WILSON

Spa Creek, 1987

There are lots of motorboaters who share the same sensitivity for the Bay and enjoyment of the water that cruising sailors do. They just choose a different kind of boat. More and more I see motorboaters that enjoy cruising when you go into remote anchorages. Years ago, it would only be sailboats there. If there was one motorboat there for the night, it would be rare.   HARVEY WALTERS

Fog on Spa Creek, 1992

Log canoe construction basically stopped in the early part of this century. As early as 1840, it was known that at St. Michaels they had races for the log canoes. That's in the newspaper. Wherever you have sailboats that are working for a living, you will have racing. First it's just one fellow's boat is faster than the other, and they make a small bet. Then you start having Fourth of July races.

Summer people come along and think this is fun, so they start financing a log canoe with a bigger rig. The sailing rig that the watermen used was conservative and small and easy to handle, but then somebody would say, "Well, I'm going to beat my brother, so I'm going to get a bigger mast," just for the race.

Then a type of canoe developed that was strictly for racing. This was back in 1885, that a canoe was built to race, not to work. Now no canoe works for a living anymore. The Log Canoe Association, I believe, has seventeen boats. Some were built for working, some for racing, but all of them have unusually large sailing rigs to take advantage of light air, and they all use hiking boards to get the crew out to windward, to balance the sail area. FRED HECKLINGER

Log canoe racing,
Tred Avon River, c. 1964

182

Camping on the Potomac River at Wynne, Maryland, 1992

When you see sailboats tied up together, those are friends who've arranged a rendezvous. They're cruising together and they anchor and they tie up together. That's very social, they're doing group sailing—rafting up, it's called. The ultimate form is a raft that is so big it becomes a big ring. You can just walk continuously from boat to boat. I'd love to go on one of those. It looks like just a continuous party. HARVEY WALTERS

Headwaters of Spa Creek,
Annapolis, Maryland,
1993

PREVIOUS SPREAD:
Chester River regatta at Love Point light, c. 1950

Every little patch of the Bay has a particularly important landmark. Some of them take on more importance as the primary navigational aid for that particular part of the Bay. Certainly Thomas Point light dominates that area around the mouth of the West River up to Tolly Point. As you get outside Annapolis harbor, that spider buoy off of Greenbury Point really takes on the same role that Thomas Point light does. It's certainly not as picturesque and doesn't evoke the same kind of feelings, but it takes on the same importance. When you get down further, Bloody Point is the same way. HARVEY WALTERS

London Town Publik House, Edgewater, Maryland, 1975

Over the eighteenth century, there was a great expansion of kinds of things that people had in their houses that made them more comfortable and more genteel. The introduction of gentility as a social standard in the Chesapeake followed what was happening in England. In wealthy households travelers often commented with astonishment that they saw the same fashions that they'd just seen in London. Even in very poor households there was a much more comfortable standard of living evident. LOIS GREEN CARR

At home on the Wicomico River,
Charles County, Maryland, 1992

188

Friends, Kent Narrows, Maryland, 1987

Two of the very difficult problems we are facing, not only here but nationally, are recreation and preservation. You are told, if you're a National Park Service person, to help the public who pay for it to use it for recreation. You're also told to preserve it for future generations. More and more, as more and more people use these facilities, these two ideas are coming in conflict, because if you have too much recreation, you wreck it. If you have less recreation, you're probably asking people to pay to preserve something which they're never allowed to use, and that isn't right, either.

Now, there's no absolute answer to recreation versus preservation. It depends where you are, what time of year you're there, and many other things. But I think it's important that the general public realize that these two ideas, both of which they support, are more and more coming in conflict in helping the people responsible work out sensible solutions to them. ROCKWOOD FOSTER

Point Lookout State Park, Maryland, 1968

Baiting a trotline, City Dock,
Annapolis, Maryland,
c. 1949

I had a trotline. If it was for crabs, it would be a ball of cord, small rope, with baits on it, and we'd have anchors at each end and buoys. We'd crab the line. We'd get our little rowboat and pick up one end of the line, and we'd work the line, and the crabs would be on there. We'd get the crabs in our boat and I'd stay in the boat in my bare feet, with the hard crabs. "Don't move your feet!" I'd never have shoes on. "Keep your feet still and the crabs won't bite." BOBBY CAMPBELL

Baiting a trotline, Tred Avon River, 1992

Rotary Club crab feast,
Annapolis, Maryland,
1990

At a crab feast, you have big boilers that you steam the crabs in. You put newspapers on the top of the table. Then you have to have crackers, and I don't mean crackers that you eat, I mean crackers that you crack the crab claws. You have to have knives to pick the backfin meat out. That is some of your equipment. We have them in the summertime when the crabs are running.

Inside we're liable to have fried chicken, and potato salad, and sliced tomatoes, and pickled beets, things that we have in the summertime that are plentiful. Corn on the cob. That is the kind of food that would go with a crab feast. ETTA W. RICHWINE

I love clams, but I get very confused. There must be as many kinds of clams as there are apples. I know there are little-necks, and there are cherrystones, and there are soft-shells, and razorbacks, but I really don't know anything about them except that I love the ones that Cantler's serves that they just call steamers. You have to be careful, because you go other places and you say you want a bucket of steamers and you might get these hard-shell steamed clams, and you get half a dozen of them on a platter instead of getting three dozen in a bucket. The kind I like are the soft-shelled ones that have that long snoot that you have to peel off. I think they're soft-shelled, and I think they're only Chesapeake Bay clams. I can remember a long time ago reading that New England, famous as it is for its clams, imported most of its clams from the Chesapeake.

HARVEY WALTERS

Shucking oysters, East New Market, Maryland, 1992

People are willing to pay more money for a Chesapeake Bay oyster. They don't have any flavor, the oysters in the South. The same way with the crabs. With the crabs, if you get real hot weather, and you get crabs out of Carolina, Louisiana, or Georgia, they've got an iodine taste and odor to them. Nothing tastes as good as a Chesapeake Bay oyster or a crab. Believe me—nothing. And I've eaten them from everywhere. Not because I was born and raised on the Chesapeake Bay and been in Maryland all my life. They just taste different.

ADRIEN HANSEN

Shucking clams, Grasonville, Maryland, 1993

Each new group either coming in or growing up sees Annapolis, Rock Hall, Crisfield, anyplace else, for the first time now. This will be their good old days. This will be their old days, at least, whether it's good or not. And it is so difficult to convey into their fundamental thinking the changes that have occurred and how different and, in many ways, how much better it used to be for the individual. They don't see it. They don't know it. It's like trying to teach kids about the Depression. They don't really believe that many people were out of work and that able-bodied people who wanted to work couldn't get a job. And the same thing is true of environmental change. So each wave that comes in starts a new baseline, and that's just getting worse and worse.
GENE CRONIN

City Dock, Annapolis, Maryland, 1981

Festival on Maryland Avenue,
Annapolis, Maryland, 1992

Some will say, "It was the good old days,"
and some will say, "Well, what was good about it?"
ELLA HARRISON

Ice cream festival, Odenton, Maryland, 1992

When I was growing up at Long Branch, we'd do like other
children and do jump-the-rope or hopscotch or hide-and-go-seek,
then we'd get on the bow of a skiff and go netting with a crabnet
and catch crabs.

We had these old-fashioned bonnets on. They felt back in
those days that if you got sunburned, it was the awfulest thing
in the world. They wanted you to look like a ghost. Even the
little babies—they'd make little bonnets for little babies when
they'd take them out. VIRGINIA EVANS

We had the best gunning in the world. We had plenty of celery that the birds would feed on and they came by the thousands. We'd set up over at Perry Point where Mill Creek runs out into the Bay. That's where they were feeding. Blue wing teal and very few other teal. Cinnamon were rare. Once in a while you would find a pair or two. That was in September. You were allowed to gun them in September. R. MADISON MITCHELL

Remington Farms, Kent County,
Maryland, c. 1963

Hunters near Remington Farms,
Kent County, Maryland, c. 1970

*We didn't pay much attention to the
limit when I started, but toward the end,
you better watch the limit because the
game wardens were watching you pretty
close. The limit when I started was
twenty-five. It was ten when I quit. Now
it's one. Not worth gunning.*
R. MADISON MITCHELL

Remington Farms, Kent County,
Maryland, c. 1970

Judging livestock,
Worcester County Fair,
Snow Hill, Maryland, 1988

Hand-milking demonstration, Somerset County Fair,
Princess Anne, Maryland, 1985

*I was in Salisbury yesterday, and you can have that. It's always,
"Move out of my way, I'm in a hurry." Over here, you just got
your own pace and leave your doors unlocked, nobody to bother
anything. Ride around in old junk cars and trucks. I just love it
here. It's inconvenient a lot of times, but it's what I like, I guess.
Bring your children up, just let 'em go and not have to worry about
'em being snatched away from you. Of course, I'm not beating the
city life. If that's what people like, that's what they like.*
LARRY MARSH

I guess I've been fishing for so long that it's second nature. I love to take people out. I never thought it could get that good where you could go out fishing and somebody will pay you money to do it. I like the old saying that a boat's a hole in the water that you throw money in—and it is. It's a canyon in the water. Boats are expensive. If you look at it on relative terms as far as what you pay to go fishing versus what you catch, you could have bought the fish a lot cheaper, but you wouldn't have the experience of going out there and trying to get them. DAVE BAUSELL

Walnut Point, Virginia, 1986

Fishing near the mouth
of the Choptank River, 1985

Fishing party near the reserve fleet, James River, 1993

For our entertainment we used to go fishing every Sunday when the rockfish was running or the trout was running or the blues. Fishing was for fun. You get up in the morning, and I'd fix this big dinner—fry chicken, make potato salad, hot biscuits, sliced tomatoes, fix crab cakes. Always had to have crab cakes, and you always had to have fried chicken. My sister would come down from Hurlock and her in-laws, and we'd all pile in the boat. We'd take our sodas and make a cake, and we'd spend the whole day out.

It's nothing in the world like that water. You became like a duck. You can't get enough of it. We'd sit there and we'd sunbathe on the cabin, and then we'd fish a while, then we'd eat a while. You'd talk to everybody next to you. And they'll say, "I think that guy down there is catching more," and we would pull up our anchor and go down and see what he was catching.

Everybody had their own fishing rod. We used to go trolling and pull those blues in two at a time. People have never lived until they've had two trout on the line or two blues on the line at one time. Boy, that's living. AUDREY ADAMS

The hot stove is kind of dwindling away now. That's something we miss. That's where everybody gathers at nighttime to tell stories after a day of crabbing. Conversations are spontaneous. There's nothing rehearsed, planned, or nothing. Somebody would come in and say somebody's sick, and you'd get on that a while. And you'd wonder how some of the other crabbers are doing, and some of them are not doing so hot. And you don't know if it's going to be an early summer or not. What I mean by early summer is one that's over with in a hurry. Early summer could be it starts early, too, there's several meanings.

But it kind of starts and drifts from one subject to another, and it all depends on the mood of the particular gang there. Sometimes they got the impotence in them and they're kind of mean-spirited. Other times, things are going good and they start telling these jokes.

They'd lean back in their chairs, "Oh, I remember one time," how it was then. That's what it is, it's bringing back the past; it keeps the past alive for the old people, to tell their experiences to the younger ones and tell them how they had it. JENNINGS EVANS

Ruke's store, Ewell, Maryland, 1991

Theodore Johnson, near Annapolis, Maryland, 1992

I've had enough water in my time. To tell you the truth, I haven't been in a boat for two years. I still eat seafood, though. I'm going to eat seafood until I pass on, 'til I can't get any more. I got to have fresh food, though. I don't eat no stale food. I go down the river 'til I see a crab hanging on to a boat, and if I got a chance, I'm going to dip him, see. I'm going to come back and I'm going to cook him today.

Nobody going to buy me seafood that came from Florida and Georgia and that kind of place. I can look at a piece of seafood and tell how old he is. You tell by the different colors he has over different parts of his body. Takes you a long while to learn that kind of stuff.
THEODORE JOHNSON

I just wish that the children today growing up could be able to relate to what the real world is all about, what the real world consists of, how beautiful the world is. If you've never ever lived close to nature and the outdoors, you haven't lived at all. You've missed something, because that's where God is. He's out there in the bushes, he's out there in the wind, he's out there with the birds and the seagulls. He's in flight twenty-four hours a day. AUDREY ADAMS

St. Mary's River, St. George Island, Maryland, 1992

PREVIOUS SPREAD:
Potomac River, 1985

The Bay used to be full of skipjacks. It's kind of heartbreaking. There used to be, I think, a hundred and some skipjacks, and now I think there's less than twenty-three. It's bad. It looks like a dying breed. And I really don't know what's going to happen next year. I don't know whether it will be worthwhile for these guys to rig up or not. Are we going to kill the last elephant before they try to figure out how to rebuild a herd? ADRIEN HANSEN

Abandoned ferry slip at Claiborne, looking toward Kent Island, Maryland, 1963

We live constantly being pulled in two directions by concerns about long-term chronic toxic sediments and the really horrible oyster situation that the Bay is in, on the one hand, and the return of eagles, the cautious but really wonderful return of rockfish, and elements that are still there of what has always made this Bay such a wonderful place. If you lose either side of that, you're losing touch with reality. Total pessimism is all wrong. Total optimism is foolish. The reality is tension. If you're really going to pay attention to it, you deal with both sides. JOHN PAGE WILLIAMS

Skipjack on rough water, c. 1953

213

Narrators

Selections from interviews with the following individuals complement the photographs:

AUDREY ADAMS was born in Fishing Creek on Hooper's Island, Maryland, in 1930. She worked alongside her husband on the water culling both oysters and crabs for twenty years. She also worked in crab-picking plants. She was interviewed at her home in Salisbury by Mame Warren on December 16, 1992.

DAVE BAUSELL was born in Hopewell, Virginia, in 1957. He was a long-distance trucker for four years; now he is a fireman in Henrico County, Virginia. He also runs a sightseeing and charter fishing business from his home on Gray's Creek in Surry. He was interviewed there by Mame Warren on July 30, 1993.

REUBEN BECKER was born in Hanover, Pennsylvania, in 1936. He is an expressionist painter who has lived on Smith Island for more than twenty years. He was interviewed at his home in Ewell by Mame Warren and Gene Cronin on November 9, 1992.

BOBBY CAMPBELL was born in Annapolis, Maryland, in 1919. Since 1947 he has been an auctioneer. He served on the Annapolis City Council during the 1950s. He was interviewed at his home by Sharie Valerio on April 4, 1990.

LOIS GREEN CARR has held the position of historian for Historic St. Mary's City since 1967. Dr. Carr was co-editor of *Maryland: A New Guide to the Old Line State* and has published widely on the colonial period of Chesapeake Bay history. She was interviewed at the Maryland State Archives by Mame Warren on August 25, 1993.

LARRY CHOWNING was born in Urbanna, Virginia, in 1949. He is a writer for the *Southside Sentinel*, field editor for *National Fisherman*, and author of *Harvesting the Chesapeake*. He was interviewed at the *Sentinel* by Mame Warren on March 29, 1993.

RAYMOND COPPER was raised in Easton, Maryland, and Philadelphia, Pennsylvania. He is the executive chef at the Tidewater Inn in Easton, where he has been employed in various capacities for twenty-eight years. He was interviewed there by Vince Leggett and Mame Warren on June 5, 1992.

TOMMY COURTNEY was born in 1945 in Leonardtown, Maryland. He holds a degree in marine biology from St. Mary's College. He is a pound net fisherman on the Potomac River and owns and operates Courtney's Restaurant in Wynne, on the St. Mary's River. He was interviewed at the restaurant by Mame Warren and Marion Warren on August 9, 1992.

GENE CRONIN was born in Harford County, Maryland, in 1917. An internationally recognized authority on marine biology, Dr. Cronin was at the Chesapeake Biological Laboratory for twenty-seven years. He later served as the director for the Chesapeake Research Consortium. He was interviewed at his home near Annapolis by Mame Warren on September 30, 1992.

DOWNES CURTIS was born in Oxford, Maryland, in 1911. He continues his lifelong craft, sewing custom-made sails with his brother Albert's assistance. He was interviewed by Mame Warren on October 30, 1992, in his sail loft in Oxford.

MARGARET MOSS DOWSETT was born in 1910 and grew up in the historic Sands House on lower Prince George Street in Annapolis, Maryland. After living away for many years as a navy wife, Mrs. Dowsett retired to Annapolis. She was interviewed at the Sands House by Mame Warren on February 9, 1990.

JENNINGS EVANS was born in Crisfield, Maryland, in 1930. Except for a few years when his father worked at the Bethlehem Steel shipyards in Baltimore during World War II, he has lived on Smith Island his entire life. Now a retired waterman, Mr. Evans was interviewed by Mame Warren and Gene Cronin in Ewell, Maryland, on November 9, 1992.

VIRGINIA EVANS was born at Long Branch on Smith Island, Maryland, in 1907. Her father, husband, and two of her sons were watermen. During both world wars her family moved to Baltimore to work in shipbuilding at Sparrows Point. She was interviewed by Mame Warren and Gene Cronin in Tylerton on November 10, 1992.

ROCKWOOD FOSTER was born in Boston, Massachusetts, in 1923. The final appointment of his long career with the American Foreign Service of the State Department was to the District of Columbia, where he headed the Department of the Environment. He has represented the District on the Interstate Commission for the Potomac River Basin for more than twenty years. He was interviewed by Mame Warren on March 31, 1993, in Washington, D. C.

BERNIE FOWLER was born in Baltimore in 1924 and grew up on Broome's Island, where he used to own Bernie's Boats. He was an early champion of the effort to clean up the Patuxent River and represented Calvert County in the Maryland Senate from 1983 to 1994. He is a member of the Chesapeake Bay Commission. Senator Fowler was interviewed by Mame Warren in his Annapolis office on July 20, 1993.

SKIPPER GARRETT was born in 1940. He is the fifth generation in his family to live at Bowler's Wharf on the Rappahannock River south of Tappahannock, Virginia. He operates Garrett's Marina there, and for some years he was involved in seeding oyster beds in Virginia waters; now he is engaged in real estate. He was interviewed on March 29, 1993, by Mame Warren in Deltaville, Virginia.

BERNARD GESSNER was born in Annapolis, Maryland, in 1905. For many years he was an executive with Coca Cola; he is now retired and lives in Edgewater. He was interviewed there by Mame Warren on April 6, 1990.

ADRIEN HANSEN was born on Hooper's Island, Maryland, in 1935. He has been a waterman and a Tidewater Fisheries marine police officer. Today he operates a seafood wholesale and catering business out of Cambridge, Maryland. He was interviewed by Mame Warren on November 4, 1992, at Deep Creek Restaurant in Arnold, Maryland.

WALTER HARRIS was born in Baltimore, Maryland, in 1919 and raised on Blooming Neck Farm overlooking the Chesapeake Bay in Kent County. He still resides there, the third generation in his family to own the farm. Originally developed as a fruit-growing operation, the farm later raised turkeys and horses. Walter Harris was interviewed by Mame Warren at Blooming Neck Farm on April 7, 1993.

EDWARD HARRISON was born in 1911 on Smith Island, Maryland. By all accounts he has caught more soft-shell crabs and peelers than any man alive. He is the son, brother, father, and father-in-law of watermen. He was interviewed by Gene Cronin and Mame Warren on November 8, 1992, at his home in Ewell.

ELLA HARRISON was born in 1918 on Smith Island, Maryland. With her husband Edward, she raised three children. She was interviewed by Gene Cronin and Mame Warren on November 8, 1992.

FRED HECKLINGER was born in Baltimore, Maryland, in 1936. A boat appraiser by profession, he has had a lifelong interest in Chesapeake Bay native craft and is a widely acknowledged expert on the subject. He was interviewed at his home near Annapolis by Mame Warren on March 10, 1993.

THEODORE JOHNSON was born in Eastport (now part of Annapolis), Maryland, in 1899. He built many houses in Annapolis and the surrounding area, as well as a few boats. He is well known as a master of marquetry, having created hundreds of pictures by an ancient method of inlaying wood. He was interviewed at his home near Bay Ridge by Mame Warren and Vince Leggett on June 26, 1992.

BRENDA HARRISON MARSH was born on Smith Island, Maryland, in 1944. She is the daughter, sister, wife, and mother of watermen. She was interviewed at her home in Ewell by Mame Warren and Gene Cronin on November 9, 1992.

LARRY MARSH was born July 22, 1956, at Rhodes Point on Smith Island, Maryland. He operates the only boat-building business and marine railway on the island. He was interviewed there on November 10, 1992, by Mame Warren.

JANICE MARSHALL was born at Ewell on Smith Island, Maryland, in 1945. She was fifteen years old when she married Bobby Marshall, a waterman. In addition to raising two children, she has served as the part-time custodian of the Tylerton school for many years. She was interviewed by Mame Warren at her home in Tylerton on December 17, 1992.

BOBBY MCKAY was born in Ridge, Maryland, in 1933. He is a second-generation waterman who works the waters near his home on St. Jerome's Creek. His son, Mark, has followed him on the water. Mr. McKay was interviewed at his home by Mame Warren on August 8, 1992.

MARIAN MCKAY was born in Valley Lee, Maryland, in 1934. She grew up on a farm, married Bobby McKay, a waterman, and raised six children in St. Mary's County. Today she manages their home-based seafood operations. She was interviewed there by Mame Warren on August 8, 1992.

R. MADISON MITCHELL was born near Havre de Grace, Maryland, in 1901. He made his career as an undertaker but gained international fame as a carver of decoys. Careful estimates indicate that he made over a hundred thousand decoys in the sixty years that he worked, probably more than any other decoy maker in the world. Some of his decoys sell today for three to five thousand dollars each. Madison Mitchell was interviewed at his home in Havre de Grace by Mame Warren and Gene Cronin on December 11, 1992. He died on January 14, 1993.

ROGER "PIP" MOYER was born in Annapolis, Maryland, in 1934 and was raised in Eastport. He served as mayor of Annapolis from 1965 to 1973. Today he is the deputy director of the Annapolis Housing Authority. He was interviewed there by Beth Whaley on May 10, 1990.

SUZANNE POGELL was born and raised in Baltimore, Maryland. She moved to Annapolis in 1978, when she was public affairs director for the Chesapeake Center for Environmental Studies of the Smithsonian Institution.

In 1984 she founded Womanship, a sailing school geared to offering women the opportunity to gain skill and confidence through boating. She was interviewed by Mame Warren in Eastport on August 30, 1993.

ETTA W. RICHWINE was raised in Culpepper, Virginia. As residents of Washington, D.C., in 1944, she and her husband bought a farm overlooking the Wicomico River in Charles County, Maryland, as a second home. For many years they raised tobacco and vegetables with the help of tenant farmers. Now a widow, Mrs. Richwine maintains the farm as a retreat from city life. She was interviewed there by Mame Warren on August 7, 1992.

ROBBIE ROBINSON was born in Prince Frederick, Maryland, in 1942. He is a fourth-generation waterman who runs a charter fishing boat out of his tackle shop on Solomons Island. He was interviewed by Mame Warren on August 26, 1992, on his boat in the middle of the Patuxent River.

PAUL SMITH was born in Nashville, Tennessee, in 1950. He moved to Virginia in 1976. Today he lives near Richmond and is a marine contractor building piers and bulkheads. He also owns and operates a cruise boat, *Pocahontas II*, on the James River out of Hopewell, Virginia, where he was interviewed by Mame Warren on July 16, 1993.

ANTHONY THOMAS was born in Hampton, Virginia, in 1954. He has worked as a waterman both offshore in the ocean and on the Chesapeake Bay. Today he is the production manager for International Seafood Company in Bena, Virginia, where he was interviewed by Mame Warren on March 30, 1993.

HAZEL T. TURNER was born near Easton, Maryland, in 1910. She was a school teacher before her marriage to Eddie Turner. She calls herself a "drylander" because she was raised on a farm. The Turner family owns a seafood-packing plant and boat-building business in Bellevue, Maryland. She was interviewed there by Mame Warren and Vince Leggett on May 29, 1992.

OTIS TURNER was born in Bellevue, Maryland, in 1906. He captained schooners for the Valliant Seafood Company for many years. Otis Turner is Hazel Turner's husband's uncle. He was interviewed by Mame Warren and Vince Leggett on May 29, 1992.

SHARIE LACEY VALERIO was born in Annapolis, Maryland, in 1941. She is a well-known actress and director on the local theater scene, and is best known as co-author and director of *The Annapolis I Remember*. She was interviewed at her home in Epping Forest by Mame Warren on March 9, 1990.

HARVEY WALTERS was born in Baltimore, Maryland, in 1942. He has been sailing out of Annapolis for more than twenty years. He is a contributing editor of *Cruising World* magazine and makes his home in northern Virginia. He was interviewed in Mayo, Maryland, by Mame Warren on August 31, 1993.

JOHN PAGE WILLIAMS was born in Richmond, Virginia, in 1942 and spent his childhood summers on the lower Potomac near Kinsale. He has run field trips for the Chesapeake Bay Foundation for twenty years utilizing workboats and canoe fleets. He writes a column for *Chesapeake Bay Magazine* and has published two books about the Bay: *Exploring the Chesapeake in Small Boats* and *Chesapeake Almanac: Following the Bay through the Seasons*. He was interviewed in the foundation's Annapolis office by Mame Warren on April 2, 1993.

WILLIS WILSON was born in Lancaster County, Virginia, near Kilmarnock Wharf in 1915. He worked on the water haul-seining fish with his father until World War II, when he went to Baltimore and worked in the shipyards. He crabbed commercially before starting up the W & E Marine Railway in Deltaville, which he still owns and operates. He was interviewed there by Mame Warren on March 29, 1993.

Photographer's Commentaries

Numerals preceding each caption refer to the page on which the photograph appears. Numerals following each caption refer to the accession number for the photograph in the Marion E. Warren Collection at the Maryland State Archives (MSA SC 1890).

Endpapers: Rhode River, 1959 MSA SC 1890-MI-2397-2

Very early in my time here on the Bay, I began to do aerial photographs. I'd never had any formal training, and I could never afford a real aerial camera, so I just used my Speedgraphic at the top shutter speed. I learned that you either had to leave the door home or be able to open the window of the airplane—and it had to be a slow airplane. Fortunately, Piper Cubs and 172 Cessnas were readily available.

And what a way to see the Chesapeake Bay! If you haven't seen the Bay from the air you have no concept of the rivers and the tributaries and how they relate to one another and how the land relates to them.

I always drove pilots nuts. We'd be headed somewhere on an assignment, and I'd look down and see a good picture. I'd nudge the pilot and motion for him to circle around to get a good angle. Some of them didn't appreciate the extra work.

Dave Scott was always great; he enjoyed finding special photographs as much as I did. I was with him when we saw this view of the Rhode River in southern Anne Arundel County. Even as I took it I thought it was a very symbolic shot of the Bay, with shadows, water, clouds, and a bit of land.

i. Sitting on the pier by Davis Creek, Bavon, Virginia, March 30, 1993

MSA SC 1890-BP-26,516

I went to Bavon, Virginia, to photograph the last of the crab dredge boats of the season. These fellows were sitting around on the pier, chatting in the afternoon. I said, "Don't move, just go ahead with your conversation."

That's one of the nice things about these watermen. You get the impression that they're stand-offish and hard for the outsider to talk to, and yet I find they're most cordial. These men couldn't have been more pleased to have their picture taken or more casual about it either.

iv. The Chesapeake Bay Bridge, July 1953 MSA SC 1890-MI-20B

When the Bay bridge opened in 1952, I immediately realized the potential for a dramatic portrait at night. It took several tries to get it right because I knew exactly where I wanted the full moon and that placement only occurs on one particular night in summer.

This picture was made from the top of the old ferry terminal—about sixty feet above ground. There was so little traffic then that I had to wait quite a while for a car to come onto the bridge. I knew it took four minutes to get across, so that's how I timed the exposure. To prevent the streak of light from being too bright in the foreground, I reached around the camera and slowly stopped the diaphragm down to f 32 as the car rounded the curve. I'm still amazed that it worked.

vi. Steward Shipyard archaeological dig near Shady Side, Maryland, May 1993 MSA SC 1890-BP-26,552

This is an archaeological dig at an old boatyard down near Shady Side. Boats were built here long before the Revolutionary War, but the boatyard has long since disappeared.

My friend Helen Orme said, "Hey, you ought to go down and see this dig." When I went down there, I found her up to her elbows in mud, sifting dirt through sieves, and anything that didn't go through the sieve was usually an object to be saved. They bag these things up and label them exactly where they found them. There's a lot of measuring going on. It takes a lot of people. They were finding all kinds of artifacts, even foundations of buildings. They were also doing some excavating out in the water, and they found a number of hulls.

Finding out the past of the Bay is as important as finding the present. The farmer who lived there had no idea that he was sitting on top of this archaeological gold mine. It's changed his life around a bit, knowing that this is there, but he was very cooperative about all those people in his field.

viii. Thomas Point light, c. 1970 MSA SC 1890-MI-2137D

This is probably my most popular photograph of Thomas Point light. It's been reproduced many times, and I call it one of my classic photographs of the Chesapeake because this was the last remaining manned lighthouse.

At the time, I had an accountant who was quite interested in what I did, and he had a powerboat. So we rode down from Annapolis to Thomas Point light and there was the sun, breaking through a bank of clouds. Being able to shoot directly into the sun let me silhouette the lighthouse. The sun also shines through the reflecting prism of the lighthouse to show that part of it. The rock piles on either side of the structure add drama.

xii–xiii. Composite of faces, 1985–1994

I took great pride while doing my Bay Project not to contrive situations or pose people. When you look at these photographs, you can see that most of the people knew I was taking their portrait. Sometimes I caught them when they were looking at me, or sometimes when they were looking off in the distance or talking in a group. Very few of these shots were strictly candid, where the people had no idea they were being photographed.

Although these pictures certainly were not taken in the controlled conditions of the studio, I consider them to be legitimate portraits. I think the subjects come off as very human, friendly, and warm because they were in their natural environment. This group represents watermen, farmers, Native Americans, merchants, teachers, homemakers, boatbuilders—the kind of people I met as I traveled around the Bay's watershed. Their faces have a lot of character, and I think that shows through in the pictures.

1. Crab potter Bill White on the James River, July 30, 1993

MSA SC 1890-BP-26,944

The boat that we were on had a flying bridge, so I was able to look down on this boat and keep things on the shoreline out of the picture. We see the shape of the boat, as well as the crab pots that are on the roof. He was very cooperative, so we could pull in as close as we wanted, which let me get a very nice close-up of what he was doing. The man was not very concerned about the camera, which is the way I like it. So often when you pull up to a boat this way, everybody stops and stares at the camera and becomes very posey.

Them Days

2. Skipjacks dredging near Kent Island, Maryland, c. 1960

MSA SC 1890-MI-820

I'd been hired by Gulf Oil Company to photograph from the air one of their new tankers going under the Chesapeake Bay Bridge. We were circling around, waiting for the tanker to get in the right position as it was coming down from Baltimore, when I looked up the way and saw these three oyster boats dredging oysters up off Kent Island. The sparkling water is really heavy waves. We were so far away they don't look that rough, but they were.

4. Lighthouse keeper, Cove Point, Maryland, October 17, 1948

MSA SC 1890-MI-12,673-9

The second year we were in Annapolis, we went down with the Annapolis Camera Club to photograph Cove Point light, and while we were there, the lighthouse keeper let us come up into the lighthouse. I made this picture of him with flash, up in the lighthouse. He was wearing his Coast Guard uniform.

This becomes a more important photograph because the lighthouse has been totally automated now. Back then, someone had to be there to check the equipment every four hours or so to make sure the radio beams were on and that the bulb in the light hadn't burned out. You didn't have the satellite communication that you have today, so people offshore would call the lighthouse to see what the tides were or to ask the depth of the water.

4. Cove Point, Maryland, October 17, 1948 MSA SC 1890-MI-1154

When I first began photographing the Chesapeake, I became intrigued by the lighthouses that lined its shores. This portrait of Cove Point light was made before the radio station and fence were erected, and it was more photogenic then. Those three windblown trees and the clouds contribute to the serenity of the scene.

5. Oyster dredging, Chesapeake Bay, 1954 MSA SC 1890-MI-71

This is the best illustration of the process of oyster dredging I've ever made. It shows action, and the dripping dredge and waves emphasize the rugged conditions watermen work in. The huge quantity of oysters on the deck indicates how things were when oysters were plentiful. Today they don't ever catch this many oysters.

I always preach that you should eliminate everything from your composition that isn't part of the message you're trying to convey. This picture is a perfect example. You have the sail, the boat, the water, the dredge, the oysters, and the people. It says all there is to say about oystering from a skipjack.

When I was growing up, there was just so much here we took a lot of it for granted. We had the oyster houses in the creeks. Even up into the eighties we had the oyster boats coming from all over because the Rappahannock was a prime oyster ground. They were some of the best on the Chesapeake as far as market-size oysters and quantity. Oystering was big time. There were a lot of oyster boats. We had buy boats here in the creek. The seafood industry played a bigger part than it does now.

LARRY CHOWNING

I shot this when I was out with Governor McKeldin inspecting the oyster fleet. We were on a powerboat moving alongside the skipjack, and I was using a hand-held 4 × 5 camera. It takes a steady hand to get the negative this sharp. When you're on a pitching boat, you have to learn how to let your body stand still and let your legs roll with the boat. There's no way you can use a tripod, you just have to learn how to do it.

6–7. Drifting dredgers, Chesapeake Bay, 1956 MSA SC 1890-MI-3032

There were still a fair number of oyster boats dredging in one location at this time. The boat would sail across the oyster bed, dragging its dredge, pulling up the oysters as it went, and then they'd throw the dredge back over and pull up another batch. When they got to the end of the bed, they would turn around and sail in the other direction. They were required to dredge under sail, and so if there was no wind, they couldn't do much dredging. On the other hand, if the wind was heavy, they would have to reef the sails. So they had quite a bit of control over it.

I was out on a Tidewater Fisheries patrol boat, covering the oyster fleet all day, just taking advantage of a free ride, when I took this one. Photographing boats is a wonderful opportunity to play with compositions because they move almost in slow motion. You just watch them drift into various formations and wait for the right moment. Sometimes it never happens.

At the time this picture was made, I didn't think it was very good. There was a slight fog and no wind—my image of oystering was full sails and lots of action. And I guess I was still influenced by dictates of the photographic salons then; the arrangement of the boats here certainly violates all of their rules of composition.

About twenty years later, I came across the negative and made a print. It turned out to be a bestseller at the gallery and has appeared on the dustjackets of three books about the Bay.

8. Waterman's gloves, Wynne, Maryland, August 8, 1992

MSA SC 1890-BP-25,920

The average person who has never seen oystering or crabbing or watermen would have no idea what these gloves were used for, but anyone who has would recognize them instantly as the rubber gloves that are worn by watermen when they're fishing, oystering, or doing anything on the water, because they're waterproof and lined. They're hanging here on the line drying. I thought it was a pretty good example of a detail of the life of a waterman.

9. Dredging oysters from a schooner, c. 1955 MSA SC 1890-MI-1261

I didn't realize that there were only one or two of these schooners still dredging oysters at the time; I photographed it mainly because it was different. It was an overcast day, so it's not an exciting, dramatic photograph, except it's a broadside of a schooner dredging oysters. I've got the dredge just being pulled over the side, so there's just no question about what's happening here. They're dredging under sail. There's no power on this boat, no engine in it. When there's a dead calm, the only way the boat can be moved is by lowering that yawl boat on the back, which has a motor, butting it up against the stern of the schooner, and pushing it.

The little lines that you see across the sails at different levels, those are reefing lines. To reef a sail, you lower it down to the boom, which is the thing that holds the sail at the bottom, and tie it around there so the sail doesn't go all the way up.

10–11. Oyster tongers, Chester River, September 25, 1986

MSA SC 1890-BP-22,302

My wife, Mary, and I were out on a four-day cruise with Jim and Debbie Wilson on their sailboat; it was early in the morning and we were just coming out of the Chester River and heading for Kent Narrows. I always had the camera out, and as we drifted by these hand tongers in the fog, I watched and waited for things to shape up. The two boats balanced by the point of land seemed like a nice composition, and when he raised the tongs, I snapped the shutter.

It's very difficult to print this negative and keep the tones right for the two dark objects in the foreground with their reflections, the misty point of land on the right side, and the barely visible land off in the distance. If I print it too dark, the fog looks dirty and grey; if I print it too light, there's no texture to the water. So it's a delicate balance in between.

The density of the print is controlled by the amount of time it's in the enlarger. The contrast is determined by the grade of paper used. I like to print this one on Kodak's No. 3 Elite paper, which means it must be developed a minimum of three to four minutes. That assures richness in the blacks.

12. City Dock, Annapolis, Maryland, November 5, 1950 MSA SC 1890-MI-425

At this time, particularly during the oyster season, a lot of skipjacks and some schooners came into Annapolis harbor to the City Dock area. I've got pictures showing them when you could walk from one boat to the other all the way across the inner harbor. Now today, if we have skipjacks in winter come into Annapolis harbor, we're very fortunate.

There are probably twenty skipjacks in this photograph, a schooner, and even a few bugeyes, tied up at the City Dock in Annapolis. This is about eight or nine o'clock on a winter morning. The masts of the boats are all different heights, the shrouds are crisscrossing one another, and in the foreground you see the tops of some of the hand-tong boats with a channel of water that goes from the right-hand side of the picture all the way out to the left and actually looks like it goes into a tunnel, which happens to be the Trumpy boatyard across the creek.

But the thing that makes this photograph even more dramatic is the sky. Dark, threatening clouds like this you only have in the wintertime. A storm cloud in the summertime does not look like this. It's a very difficult negative to print because you have so much dark area; holding the detail in the boats is quite creative printing.

There are no patent-tong boats in this picture, but today it's mostly patent-tong boats and a few hand-tong boats that come into Annapolis in the wintertime, and almost no skipjacks, and of course no bugeyes, so this becomes a very historic photograph as well as a dramatic picture.

In the foreground are some hand-tong boats, and the reason I say that is, there are the hand tongs lying on the deck of the boat.

13. Oyster bounty, Annapolis, Maryland, c. 1948 MSA SC 1890-MI-823

The first winter we were in Annapolis I shot this great pile of oysters on a buy boat as she came into the Annapolis harbor. You can see another, smaller boat coming in out in the distance. You look over to Eastport and there's almost nothing over there, at least not in comparison to what is there today.

But I think the strongest thing about this picture is the great pile of oysters. There are many, many bushels of oysters, much more than you would catch in any one day today. And the other thing is, they don't bring many oysters into Annapolis City Dock anymore because there are no oyster houses there now. Back in 1948, the Chesapeake Seafood House was where the parking lot is today near the harbor master's office. You could watch them unload oysters and then take a bushel of them down to Schley's at the Market House and they would open them for you.

13. Unloading oysters, Solomons Island, Maryland, c. 1960

MSA SC 1890-BP-1256

This was a small haul of oysters for back then. They've got a pulley with a bucket. They load the bucket on the boat and pull it up, and then they dump the bucket into a wheelbarrow on shore. You can see by the size of the men's hands that those are good-sized oysters. There are three boats here, and two of them are draketail oyster boats. This was a common scene anywhere there was an oyster house.

14. City Dock, Annapolis, Maryland, 1949 MSA SC 1890-MI-534

This was the pier used for unloading oysters from buy boats at City Dock. It didn't last too much longer after this photograph was made. In the distance are Horn Point and the ram *Edwin and Maud*. The ram was once a lumber and bulk-cargo carrier, but by this time she had been converted into a pleasure boat that took passengers on week-long cruises on the Bay. Later she was taken to Maine and her name was changed to *Victory Chimes*.

My daughter Mame used this picture on the cover of *Then Again*, her book about Annapolis during the years 1900–1965. It seemed to symbolize that bygone era in the sleepy waterfront community that Annapolis was before all the tourists arrived.

15. Annapolis, Maryland, from Eastport, 1949 MSA SC 1890-MI-536A

After we moved to Annapolis, I always went out on snowy days looking for good views, and that's when I found this vantage point on Spa Creek. I knew I needed to get above the six-foot-high sea grass in the foreground, so I piled up a bunch of wooden crates that had been dumped in this vacant lot. Then I climbed up with my tripod and film holders and set up the camera twelve feet above the ground.

I used the rear element of a triple convertible lens to make the picture, and when I climbed down, I couldn't find the other piece. About a week later, when the snow melted, the neighbors called me and said they'd found it, so I gave them a print of the picture.

My husband would take and put the tongs overboard, which was two sticks with wire-like teeth. He'd open them up like a pair of scissors. When he'd close them up, that meant he had oysters. He would lift them up and throw them on a board. It was about three feet wide and the whole width of the boat. We call it a culling board. So I would stand there, and I'd take a hammer. I would chip off the little baby oysters and throw them back. Then I'd pick the legal size and throw them in the bottom of the boat. AUDREY ADAMS

16–17. Crisfield, Maryland, c. 1957 MSA SC 1890-MI-1287

Once upon a time, Crisfield was known as the seafood capital of the world. It still is, really. I have pictures taken along the shoreline of Eastport, in Annapolis, that don't look much different from this. There were always handbuilt piers. A guy could take his little hand pile driver, and go out there and drive his own piles with any kind of wood he wanted, as deep as he wanted or as shallow as he wanted. He could build it with scrap lumber; he could do anything he wanted.

Those days are gone forever now. You have to get a permit. Regulations have cleaned up the whole act. So this becomes an important picture because it is of a period when you didn't have that kind of regulation.

Back in the mid-fifties to late fifties, the Maryland Port Authority developed Somers Cove down in Crisfield. They were going to have it be a second major port of Maryland, after Baltimore, to rejuvenate the town. It really turned out to be more of a sport fishing center than anything else, and it's a fairly good-sized yacht basin now. Every year they hold the Crab Derby on Labor Day weekend, and that brings in thousands and thousands of people.

To Crisfield from Route 13, which is about twelve miles, the road is just as straight as a die. You can almost put your car on auto-drive and lie back and go to sleep, and you wind up in Crisfield. You drive right through the wetland. I wonder whether they would be able to get away with that today, disturbing that much wetland.

18. Capt. George Hallock and his monster crab, Whitehall Creek, near Annapolis, Maryland, c. 1950 MSA SC 1890-MI-12,674-1

I was at a friend's house about forty years ago when George Hallock came up with this huge crab and said, "Isn't this the largest crab you ever saw?" I had to agree that it was, so I got my camera and made his portrait. I really took the picture just to please him, but now it's an example of what crabs used to be like.

I remember asking Captain Hallock to raise his knee so that his pose would be casual, like his attire. I used a flash that overpowered what daylight was left and gave the picture a dark background.

19. Rockfish party, near Annapolis, Maryland, c. 1952 MSA SC 1890-MI-883

This picture was taken in the early fifties when the Chesapeake Bay Fishing Fair was held in Annapolis. I was the official photographer for the fair, so I wanted to get some good shots of sport fishing in the area. I went out on a powerboat and we approached this boat and asked if these people had caught anything. "No," they said, "fishing's been bad."

We explained that we weren't the marine police and that we were trying to show off great fishing in the Bay. They pulled out a couple of good-sized rockfish, so I teased them that I needed more for a really good picture and out came all of these over-sized fish. See, back in those days there was a maximum-size limit on rockfish. You had to throw back the really big ones because those were supposed to be the good ones for spawning more fish. Now, of course, a scene like this is a nostalgic record of the days when rockfish were plentiful and people took them for granted.

20–21. Peeler shanty, Smith Island, Maryland, July 1965

MSA SC 1890-SI-128 (35 mm)

One of the things that I like about this picture is that it captures a good feel of the rural—and I do mean rural—existence of Smith Island. There's nothing but marsh grass, wetlands, as far as the eye can see, and one pole way off in the distance. You see a lot of baskets that are for crabs, you see a man in his suspenders and a white shirt, and you see the isolation and desolation of living on the island. The man is just sort of standing there, bent over a little bit, his eyes looking off in the distance, as though he may be waiting for the boat to come in.

I think you get a feeling almost as though you're there, and that's, I think, what a photograph is supposed to do. You feel like you have gotten, as a viewer, a little experience about the man and his life and the way he lives.

21. Sorting peelers, Smith Island, Maryland, July 1965

MSA SC 1890-SI-132 (35 mm)

I went down to Smith Island for the first time in the early sixties to photograph a story for the *New York Times*. When I came back, I had about ten rolls of film, so that's well over three hundred pictures. One of the advantages of 35 mm over a larger format, although I now feel I can do the same thing in 120, is that it's spontaneous.

I walked up to this man and he was sorting crabs, and I just pointed the camera and took pictures. I backed off enough to show the baskets that he was sorting from and the

three houses in the background, which are typical Smith Island–type houses, and on the right the window of the church.

He's sorting peeler crabs out of the day's catch. They're going down here in a floater box. You can see one down here in the water. They swim around in there until they peel their shells, and then with a dip net, he takes those crabs back out and they're soft-shells. You can tell by the coloration on part of the shell whether it's going to peel within the next few days.

Now this whole operation of shedder boxes is up on the land, and the water is pumped up out of the Bay and it drains back into the Bay again. You can do that in a covered shed, and a woman can do it or a man can do it without getting out into a dinghy. So it's a much smoother operation, and obviously the sun is kept off the shedding crabs, which helps protect them. These old homemade wharfs are gone now, so this is a very strong record of an era that is past on Smith Island.

22. General store, Ewell, Maryland, July 1965 MSA SC 1890-SI-496 (35 mm)

This place has changed hands and now is a restaurant and general store. The building is very much the same except the sign has changed. The same tin-roof porch is there. The main thing I like about this is the casualness of all the men standing around talking.

You've got a guy hugging a pole—leaning on it—and two other guys leaning on another of the porch poles, and four people sitting, just listening. You get a very natural feeling of life on the island and the natives conversing with one another. It also shows enough of the structure of the building that you get a feeling of the atmosphere around them and not just a close-up of the men themselves.

Middleton, Dize, and Evans are among the most prominent families on Smith Island, and there are a lot of intermarriages. I remember talking to one man and asking him his name, and it was not any of those names, and I said to him, "Oh you're not from Smith Island." He looked at me and said, "How do you know?" and I said, "Well, your name isn't one of those three." And he said, "But I'm married to a Dize." So that took care of that.

23. Boardwalk, Smith Island, Maryland, July 1965 MSA SC 1890-SI-252 (35 mm)

Of all the pictures I made on my first trip to Smith Island, this is my favorite because it really, in one picture, shows the solitude and the isolation of the island. It shows a homemade plank walkway out to a couple of crab houses. At the end of it is a boat tied up, and you can see water beyond it, but most of it is marsh grass, and on either side of the walkway there are two small buildings. They're identical, and they're crab houses where they store the crab pots and baskets and sort crabs out of the sunlight.

This was taken with a wide-angle lens, and it looks like it's a long way out there, and you see nothing else across the horizon at all. A woman walked out with a box of crabs, and I let her get out to the end. She gives scale to the photograph.

These walkways are gone now. I went back recently looking for it and couldn't find any evidence of this scene.

Working the Water

24. Hand tonging for oysters at the mouth of the Severn River,
c. 1953 MSA SC 1890-MI-2117

This was back in the early fifties and it was taken out off Bay Ridge. You see the hand tongs being brought up out of the water with oysters in the tongs. The second tonger is just dumping his catch onto the culling board, and it's gotten pretty full. They're going to have to stop and cull those oysters or they're going to start falling over the side.

It's awfully hard to manage the tongs because you have to lower them all the way to the bottom and clinch them closed and bring them up closed, and wet, and in the winter the water's cold, icy sometimes, and so it's very rugged work. You see they're both wearing gloves. Tonging is much easier in shallow water, but sometimes the best oysters are in deeper water. It's not an easy way to make a living.

26. Culling oysters on the Choptank River, c. 1955 MSA SC 1890-MI-2115

Now here's a man culling oysters on his culling board; he's brought them up with his hand tongs, and the board is heaped high with oysters. What he's doing with this little hammer is sorting out good oysters that are legal size and quality oysters, throwing them in the bottom of the boat, and shoving everything else overboard. This was very cold weather because there are icicles in the photograph. When you see icicles, you know he was working below freezing, because this is salt water so it has to be a couple degrees colder to freeze.

219

The UHF radio, that's really funny to listen to. Everything gets talked over in the morning. It functions differently than it would in most places. It's communication on another level. A lot of decisions are made because of what's said on the radio. On a windy morning, I'll turn on the radio and one person will say, "Well, are you going to go out?" And the other will say, "Well, I don't know, I heard it's supposed to stay windy all day." And somebody in town will say, "Well, it's not too windy down here." And the last word will be, "Well, if nobody else is going out, neither am I." And the radio goes dead for the morning. REUBEN BECKER

I think this was down in the Choptank River. He's culling right over the oyster bed because he's replanting the shells and small oysters right back where he got them. Oysters live in beds; they don't live just all over the Bay. Replanting the small oysters so they can grow another year is very important.

27. Andrew Wright, Kent Narrows, Maryland, November 1990

MSA SC 1890-BP-24,433

I met this fellow the first time I stopped to photograph watermen at Kent Narrows, but he didn't want to have his picture taken. When I went back the next time, I took prints of the portraits I'd taken of the other men and showed them to him and said, "Don't you want to be part of this, too?" This time he said, "Sure." His gold tooth was an unexpected bonus; I didn't see it until I got into the darkroom.

I always chat with the watermen first, asking about this year's catch, the weather, or whatever. It takes a while; you can't just point a camera at someone and expect to get much—you have to win their confidence.

27. Oyster tongs, City Dock, Annapolis, Maryland, March 4, 1987

MSA SC 1890-BP-22,486

This is looking down on a portion of two hand-tong boats. In the foreground, you see the wheel of the boat. You see two sets of hand tongs; they're lying on a culling board. Then off in the upper corner is a pair of rubber gloves.

This was taken down at City Dock in Annapolis. I've always contended, when I've spoken at camera clubs, that in the wintertime—although it's not quite as true today as it used to be—there are so many oyster boats in there that you could go there anytime when the boats are in, particularly on a weekend, and you could do ten outstanding photographs on any one day. There are just so many interesting designs to be had.

This picture could have been made in Oxford, it could have been made on Deal Island, it could have been made at Solomons. These boats are everywhere on the Bay.

28–29. Hand tonger at sunrise, Tilghman Island, Maryland, March 5, 1987 MSA SC 1890-BP-23,269

I got up at sunrise and went down to the dock and I saw this deadrise coming out from Knapps Narrows, so I waited and just got the one exposure. If you can look into the sun directly, you can also take pictures of it. The sun flared very nicely. I balanced the composition of the channel markers with this boat coming out and the wake of the boat. Fortunately, the man was standing on the stern of his boat, silhouetted, which added more drama to it.

You know he's going out to do oystering. Anybody who knows Bay boats would know this is a workboat, and the giveaway is the hand tongs stacked on the deckhouse of the boat.

This is one of my favorite pictures of the Bay because it is so well balanced between the workboat and the sunlight and the pilings. It's very backlighted and very dramatic. I made it with a Hasselblad. It probably would have been difficult to do with a large-format camera because of the timing. As I get older, the bigger camera is a little harder to hold.

29. Bennett Point, Maryland, March 31, 1986 MSA SC 1890-BP-20,653

You don't often see women on the boats, but here's a woman down at the dock and they're all having a conversation. The people were not aware they were being photographed, and they're standing there very casually, probably talking over the day's catch.

Over on the boat you see oysters. You see the dock with a pulley rig, which is what they use if they bring oysters in in larger containers.

29. Robbie Robinson, Solomons, Maryland, May 2, 1992

MSA SC 1890-BP-25,519

This is our friend Robbie Robinson. I was attending a conference at Solomons, and during a break in the conference, I went out with a camera to see what was going on by the water. I was taking some pictures of rockfish being cleaned, when this fellow steps up to me and asks me what I was taking pictures for. He said he had a charter boat and he would be glad to take us out fishing anytime we wanted to. I said, "Well, gee, we'll take you up on that." He gave me a card, and I said, "Hey, you're a handsome guy. How about posing for a photograph?"

So he posed here for the photograph, with his *Miss Regina II* cap on; *Miss Regina II* is his boat. I think it's a very nice portrait of a charter captain. When we did take him up on his offer, it was summertime and the beard was gone. He shaves it off when it gets hot.

30–31. *Robert L. Webster* dredging oysters, c. 1953 MSA SC 1890-MI-873

This was taken when I was going out doing a lot of oyster pictures. This is the *Robert L. Webster* from Deal Island, and her decks are just absolutely loaded with oysters.

I very carefully waited for that schooner to get to where it was in the composition with the *Webster*. Otherwise, she would be way off from it and I'd have to include too much. Fortunately, the skiff was being pulled along, and I put it into the composition as the lead end of the boat. As you see, the water's pretty rough, and we've got an overcast sky. But it's mostly a very dramatic picture of how many oysters they have on the boat.

32. Dredging oysters near the eastern side of the Chesapeake Bay Bridge, c. 1958 MSA SC 1890-MI-1773

I'm on a skipjack near the Bay bridge, and these two men are pulling up the dredge, just breaking the water, pulling the oysters up on the culling board. They're going to sort out the oysters and put the culls back overboard as they drag for another haul of oysters.

The young oysters spawn on old shells. Fact is, I've gone out when they've hauled up old, old oyster shells by the boatload and taken them and dumped them into where they want new oyster beds in order to give the spawn—little oyster spawn—someplace to hang onto to grow into oysters. Oysters also love old tires as spawning ground. Now what they do is take these tires and plant them in a tub of concrete, upright, and the concrete, of course, sinks and sits on the bottom and the oysters can grow all over the tire.

32. Watermen at Kent Narrows, Maryland, November 1990

MSA SC 1890-BP-24,494

I watched these men talking for about ten minutes before I began taking pictures. I wanted to get the right relationship between the men and the boats in the background. I was also waiting for the young man on the left to look up and seem involved in what was going on. I guess he's really why I took the picture.

I have their names, but I don't really know who these men were; I assume they were all working on the water that day. I liked the University of Maryland sweatshirt—it seemed like a nice commentary. You don't usually see watermen wearing university sweatshirts, so I assume he was a student home on vacation helping out his buddies who work as watermen.

33. Peewee Bozman cooking aboard his workboat on Deep Creek, off the Magothy River, November 30, 1992 MSA SC 1890-BP-26,330

This man was cooking for the crews of several boats. He had a big skillet of potatoes that he was frying on a little stove. Down in the cabin there isn't much room, so he's got to be pretty efficient. He's built a little shelf to hold things alongside the stove. They live on these boats all week long.

We asked him if they cooked much seafood, and he said occasionally they'll catch a fish and cook it, but they mostly go to the grocery store. I can remember when a lot of the skipjacks came in to Annapolis and the A&P and the Acme were still there. All they had to do was just walk across the street to buy their supplies.

34–35. Buy boats on the Magothy River near the mouth of Deep Creek, April 1, 1969 MSA SC 1890-MI-2558-1

The oystermen, when they dredge oysters, pile them on the deck. If the weather is a little warm, oysters don't keep too long, and so they bring them to the buy boat. As the name implies, the buy boat buys the oysters from the oystermen and then takes them to Baltimore or to a major packing house. So these buy boats were a very common thing on the Chesapeake Bay. The oyster boats could go back to oystering very quickly, and it was an efficient way to get the oysters in to port.

This was probably the last of an era. So many of the skipjacks have disappeared. When there are only three or four skipjacks, it certainly doesn't pay for a buy boat to go out and wait all day for what oysters they can collect. Now the oystermen come back to their home port, like Crisfield or Annapolis, and unload their oysters onto a truck. So the need for the buy boat is passing. There are still a few around, but I don't think there are any in the Magothy anymore.

35. Buy boat at City Dock, Annapolis, Maryland, December 8, 1992

MSA SC 1890-BP-26,350

This used to be a common sight in Annapolis, to see a buy boat lying off the City Dock in Spa Creek, buying oysters from the oyster boats as they came in from tonging.

There aren't many buy boats around any more, but last fall, this buy boat was there. The buy boat is distinctive by the pulleys, the hoists, and also the square cabin.

The man on the oyster boat is passing a big bucket by pulley up onto the buy boat. He will be paid in cash for his catch. Then he goes on his way, and another boat pulls up into that position. Sometimes there are two or three boats idling out there, waiting their turn to unload their oysters. The next night I went down again, and the buy boat was tied up by the Fleet Reserve Club. They had a conveyor belt and were unloading oysters onto a truck.

36. Soft-shell clamming operations near Kent Island, Maryland, August 1959 MSA SC 1890-MI-2434

This was a picture that I made, for the seafood industry of Maryland, of clamming on Kent Island just south of the Bay bridge. This was made as a color slide and converted to black and white. I have never been able—and I find few photographers can, particularly on spontaneous things this way—to work both black and white and color at the same time. But in this particular period of time, color was what was wanted, and for many years there, I'd say, black and white was not being used that much. Everybody wanted color, so you photographed everything in color, and if you needed it in black and white, which was a rare occasion, you converted it to black and white.

There is a slight difference in the quality of the picture between what would have been made originally on black and white film versus the conversion. There's no question that it would have been better to have made this picture directly in black and white, but the need at that time was for color.

This picture illustrates clam dredging fairly well. There's a conveyor belt that is being driven by a chain, and it's pulling the soft-shell clams up out of the bottom. The conveyor belt has a jet of water that, when it's lowered to the bottom of the Bay, pushes whatever is in front of the jet of water onto the conveyor belt, and the conveyor belt brings it up. These two men are sorting out the clams and leaving shells, bricks, pieces of metal, pieces of wood, whatever happens to come up, to go back over the side into the water. The good clams are being sorted out by hand into the basket and set over on the side, and you see at least a dozen full, heaping baskets of clams in the background of the photograph. So obviously clamming was pretty good at this time.

Any time you see a rig either at the dock or out in the water with this conveyor belt on the side of it, you know it's a clam boat, and the clam boats, in contrast to an oyster boat, have a horizontal canopy over them to block the sun.

36. Hard-shell clamming on the James River, July 30, 1993

MSA SC 1890-BP-26,966

Down in the James River, they use different rigs for clamming than they do in Maryland. In Maryland they use a conveyor belt to bring up the soft-shell clams, but in Virginia they use a scissors-type lift to harvest hard-shell clams. This has to be done in reasonably shallow water.

We found these clam boats in quite a lot of locations on the James River. I don't think I've ever seen as many clam boats at one time. They were out in the morning when we went by on our way to Norfolk, but when we came back at mid-afternoon, there wasn't a clam boat or a crab boat in sight. If they took the clams in at six o'clock and had to put them in a storage bin overnight, the clams would lose a lot of their freshness.

Down near Norfolk, seeing all the industrial activity, you just automatically think about pollution. I think if you went into the store and they said, "These clams were caught from the lower James outside Newport News Shipbuilding," you might turn them down, because you'd think that has to be polluted water. But the health inspectors obviously inspect these clams, so they must be all right for market.

37. Transporting clams, c. 1960 MSA SC 1890-MI-1718

I haven't done a great deal on soft-shell clams on the Bay, but on the other hand, it's not a big industry either, in comparison to oystering and crabbing. This was done several years before Hurricane Agnes, and Gordon Hallock, the head of seafood marketing for Maryland, said a lot of our clams were shipped to New England to be relabeled and sent back as New England clam chowder. He bragged that we had an absolutely endless supply of soft-shell clams. The clams were so thick that we had a hundred-years' supply right there on the bottom of the Chesapeake Bay, that no matter what happened to oystering and to crabbing, the clams would be there, and we had to develop this clamming industry to be a major industry in Maryland.

Well, Hurricane Agnes came down, flooding the Susquehanna, bringing a tremendous amount of fresh water into the Chesapeake Bay, altering the salinity of the water. It almost wiped out the clam industry entirely. It's never recovered in all the years since then. So here was something that nature just about wiped out in one fell swoop.

A picture like this is a difficult photograph to print because you have people in the shade in the foreground and people in bright sunlight out in the background; and to dodge and print the detail into the background without it being obvious, as well as not losing the detail in the foreground, makes it a real darkroom challenge.

38–39. Crab potter Bill White on the James River, July 30, 1993

MSA SC 1890-BP-26,940

This was down in the lower James River, and this man was running his crab pots. He probably has a license to crab commercially since he has so many crab pots on the awning of his boat. This is not a typical Maryland crab boat. It's a little different than the design we see up here.

40. Crab scrape boat, Rhodes Point, Smith Island, Maryland, November 10, 1992 MSA SC 1890-BP-26,238

I was wandering around Rhodes Point when I saw this Jenkins Creek crab scrape boat, obviously very well maintained at a good dock, and it shows the whole rigging very clearly. The scrape is thrown over the side and let out, and while the boat moves along at a very slow speed, it scrapes over the grasses, and the crabs, who are hiding in the grass so they can shed, are pulled into the net. Then it's pulled back up on the washboard and dumped out. The crabs are sorted as to how near they are to shedding, and the small ones are thrown back. You would never see a scraping boat like this on the Western Shore. It's a very shallow draft boat with no keel.

41. Don Cawood and Keith Thomas, Deal Island, Maryland, September 1, 1988 MSA SC 1890-BP-22,100

I actually posed these fellows. They seemed to be classic watermen types, and they were wearing the watermen's uniform: baseball-style caps. In warm weather, most of them wear white T-shirts like the guy on the left. They were standing by a caged-in area where twenty or so peeler boxes were located—their operation for managing peeler crabs as they shed their shells.

It seemed to me that the sign indicated pride in their work more than real advertising. The S on the sign was falling down, so I fixed it before I asked them to pose. Although I usually don't like to alter the original scene, if I'd left it dangling, it would have been a distraction from the personalities, who were the real subject of the photograph.

42. Repairing crab pots, Wenona, Maryland, April 1, 1991

MSA SC 1890-BP-24,871

There's quite a bit of repair work that has to be done to crab pots before they're put out. Crabbers check to see that their crab pots haven't rusted away and that their gates open because once they get the pots out in the water, they've got to pull them in fast and dump them fast, and everything has to work well.

This fourteen-year-old boy was cleaning out the debris and patching the wiring on these crab pots. He and his brother and his father were all working at it. This was taken in the spring, and it's one of the few pictures I've got of a young boy working. Rarely have I seen any children out working. Whether it's been my timing, or whether the children don't get involved with parents' work, I don't know.

42. Crab pot floaters, St. Jerome's Creek, August 8, 1992

MSA SC 1890-BP-25,874

This is a group of floaters for crab pots and they're piled on a pier on St. Jerome's Creek. I turned a couple of them so they pointed in instead of out and made this picture.

Each crabber who sets out crab pots has his own set of numbers and his own colors and also different shapes, so that when you come to a whole series of these floaters in the water, you know they're his. You can't say, "Oh, I pulled up your crab pots by mistake." It's just like identifying any other property.

Crab potters come along in their boats with a hook, hook the floater, pull it in, and then pull up the rope and haul the crab pot up on the boat, empty the crabs out, bait it again and throw it back overboard. It won't be in the same spot, but the floater will show where it is.

43. Crab skiff docking at Saxis, Virginia, July 1, 1989 MSA SC 1890-BP-22,718

This is an old Virginia boat, and it's a little different than a boat that's from Maryland. Each area developed their own style of boat for the depth of the water and the amount of marshland they went through. This old man was seventy-two years old, and he was

I remember one time when Morris was on his way home, I was making bread. All of a sudden, this awful feeling came over me. It was around one o'clock in the afternoon, and there was a terrible storm that day, and I got down on my knees right in the kitchen, and I said, "Lord, I've got this awful feeling. I know there's something wrong, and I don't know what it is. I just wanted to ask you to take care of it." In about a half hour's time, Morris walked in the door. He'd almost turned over coming in the jetty. BRENDA HARRISON MARSH

bringing in a load of crabs to Saxis, which is down on the Eastern Shore peninsula of Virginia.

I probably walked ten or fifteen steps one way or the other on the dock to get the boat the way I wanted it. I was trying to tell a story of the shape of this boat, what he had on it, and the man, and keep other things out of the picture.

He was coming in to the dock, so I only had an instant in which to make all my judgments as to when to take the photograph. I'm on the dock looking down into the boat, which helps a lot. He's holding a line that goes out to a pulley and then to the rudder, so he can steer from right where he's standing.

43. Joe Kitching, Smith Island, Maryland, July 28, 1991

MSA SC 1890-BP-25,136

Joe Kitching was a seventy-six-year-old crabber who was out scraping for soft-shell crabs. The crab wants to protect himself from being captured or eaten by predators, so he gets down into the grasses to shed. Smith Island is about the only remaining place in Maryland where you've got all this marsh grass, so this is about the only place left where you can go out and catch the soft-shell crabs from the sea grass.

This photograph has pretty dull lighting on it, but those are the conditions that I had and everything can't be bright and sunny. I like it for the texture of the man and the fact that he's holding this pole.

44–45. Tending shedding boxes, Taylor's Island, Maryland, c. 1987

MSA SC 1890-BP-20,036

The trained eye can tell when crabs are about to shed. It's only about four hours that they're really soft-shell crabs of peak condition, so they have to be tended several times a day, at least, and shifted from one float to another.

They pump the water out of the Bay into these boxes and let it drain back out; the crabs are continually moving in fresh water. I kidded the woman who was tending this operation and said, "This is something now that you can do that the men don't have to do," because they used to do it from a little skiff, and usually it was the men who did that. Of course, this is much more efficient and much faster. In many of the bigger shedding houses today, these floats have a roof over them, which makes it cool in the summertime, but having this operation so visible worked out well for this picture.

45. Waterman keeping records, Saxis, Virginia, August 1989

MSA SC 1890-BP-23,085

This is an important picture because it shows the lifestyle of the waterman. This man is keeping records in his crabhouse—the place where they pack the soft-shell crabs for shipping. He sells only to wholesalers who take the product out on trucks. I tried to buy some soft-shells directly from him but he wouldn't do it. He said it would complicate his bookkeeping.

This man was one of two brothers who had crabbed here for forty years. The calculator is probably new, but everything else has stayed pretty much the same for all those years. I wanted to show the rustic construction and all the details in the background. In a scene like this, everything relates to the action. This man is seventy years old; when he goes, this way of life will probably go with him.

46. Southern Maryland, c. 1957 MSA SC 1890-MI-10,354 (35 mm)

I took this picture a long time ago, back when I first started using a 35 mm format. I got my first Leica in 1956. My Aunt Edna was working for the State Forestry Department at the time, and we were on an expedition with two foresters looking for the largest specimen trees in the state. We knew one of the big trees was in the vicinity, so we stopped to ask this woman where it was.

The woman was completely unaware that I was taking her picture. I was in the back seat of the car and just quietly pointed the camera at her when she turned to look in the direction of the tree. I've always been struck by the children here; the little girl seems defiant, as though she doesn't trust these outsiders, while her younger brother seems more accepting of strangers.

A picture like this was probably influenced by the Farm Security Administration photographers of the generation before me. When I was just getting started in this business, a Kodak representative told me that I was too late, that everything had already been photographed. I don't believe it. Yes, Dorothea Lange may have made pictures of impoverished women and children, but that takes nothing away from the dignity of this family and the necessity to record their lives.

46–47. Storm off Smith Island, Maryland, July 26, 1991

MSA SC 1890-BP-25,071

I was on a moving boat and shooting a very slow shutter speed for the simple reason that the light was so weak. There was a threatening cloud and within five minutes after I made this picture, it was raining torrents. I had to put the camera up in the bow of the boat under cover, and we got soaked coming back in.

48. Bobby, Marian, Gary, and Mark McKay, Ridge, Maryland, August 8, 1992 MSA SC 1890-BP-25,887

We discovered the McKay family on an excursion to St. Mary's County. When they had finished bringing in the day's crabs, I said I'd like to do a family group. As the older boy, the waterman, came in with the dolly, I said, "Why don't you just wait right there?" He said, "Okay," and he leaned on one of the pilings with one arm on the dolly. So I brought the rest of the family down and I put his younger brother behind him, and his mother behind the dolly, and when his father got his position, what did he do? He put an arm up on the stack of crab pots, so it gave it a very natural appearance. It's obvious they're posing, but on the other hand, they're posing in a relaxed way. The light was very poor, but that's good for this photograph because we can see into the shadows quite nicely and we have a background of the water behind them.

The younger boy, Gary, said he was interested in computers. I asked him whether he wanted to go out on the water, and he said he wanted no part of it. Interesting thing, the uniform of the waterman is a solid-colored T-shirt. Here, the father's wearing a white T-shirt and the son is wearing a dark T-shirt, but the boy who doesn't want to be a waterman has a striped shirt on.

49. Crab dredge boat, Davis Creek, March 30, 1993 MSA SC 1890-BP-26,541

This is a crab dredge boat coming in to dock. Here's a channel marker, number 10, with an osprey nest on top of it and an osprey sitting there. I would like to have been a little lower so that the osprey would have stood out against the sky, but it was impossible to get there, particularly with the speed of the boat coming in. On the other hand, had I gotten lower, the channel marker would have dominated the boat or at least have been of equal value. This way, it takes secondary importance to the boat itself.

In taking these kinds of photographs, your timing has to be perfect because if the boat were back ten feet, it would be one subject and your channel marker would be another subject. If it were too close to the channel marker, it would look like it was tied up there. So you have to judge the instant when it's close enough to make it part of the composition and yet not too close.

Those stains on the side of the boat show where the dredge has been pulled over the side. You actually see the dredge sitting there, too. We saw two types of dredge boats. The other type had a much bigger dredge off the stern of the boat.

Many of the female crabs go down to the mouth of the Bay to hibernate for the winter and to spawn. Maryland watermen feel that digging them out of the mud takes a big percentage of the crabs before they spawn and therefore cuts into the crop. The Virginia waterman says, "Oh, there are so many eggs there that very few of them get up the Bay anyway, so what we take doesn't really affect it." I've heard that for years and years, and it's a standoff of opinion.

49. The last dredged crabs of the season, Bavon, Virginia, March 30, 1993 MSA SC 1890-BP-26,543

This is the end of March, and these crabs have been dug out of the bottom in Virginia waters. In Maryland, crabs normally are packed in bushel baskets; here it's a different type of container and really a whole different technique. This bin holds at least twice as many crabs as a basket.

The last container they unloaded had just clams and conchs in it. When they dredge the bottom, they're going to pick up whatever is there, and these men sorted out a full container of conchs and clams. This whole scene has an end-of-the-day appearance to it, which is what it was—the sun was going down and the crabs were being unloaded to be put on a truck and taken away to the market.

When they run the trotlines and crab pots in the upper Bay, they're usually in by noon. They're catching them near the surface of the water and, as the day goes on, the crabs don't eat, and there's no point in being out there. So they catch them in the early part of the day and come home. Here it's late in the day, so this means that the time of day doesn't affect the dredging of crabs. These crabs are down at the bottom, and they don't know what time of the day it is, or care.

I don't know how this affects the marketing of them; I guess these crabs have to go somewhere and be stored for the night. If they're brought in in the middle of the day, the crabbers have all afternoon to dispose of them through the marketplace.

The James River is divided up, particularly on the lower James, into some fairly large pieces of property—the old plantations—so it hasn't been subdivided. The shoreline is either low and marshy or high bluff. You don't see the residential development that you see on a lot of creeks and lakes. There's plenty of marshes and mudflats. If you're not in the dredged channel, chances are you're in knee-deep water or less. Even though the river may be two miles wide, it's only deep in the dredged channel that the Corps keeps maintained for shipping traffic. PAUL SMITH

50. Steaming crabs, Pope's Creek, Maryland, c. 1963

MSA SC 1890-MI-383 (35 mm)

I knew slot machines were on their way out, so I went down to Pope's Creek in Charles County to document the last of them. I was shooting away when I looked through the kitchen door and saw this guy steaming crabs. He never even knew I took his picture.

That's the advantage of 35 mm—you're not so obvious. It used to be easier to get candid shots like this before everyone had cameras because most people didn't pay attention if you didn't use a flash. This was a guess exposure; I used Tri-X film every day, so I never had to use a meter and could usually judge the light levels with confidence.

51. Crab pickers, Kent Island, Maryland, August 8, 1963

MSA-SC-1890-MI-12,677-4

I took this picture back when I was doing an exhibit about how seafood was processed for the Maryland Tidewater Fisheries people. No one has figured out how to pick crabmeat mechanically as well or as thoroughly as hand pickers do it. The people who've been doing it for years really know how to remove all the pieces of shell, and they take pride in their work.

Natural light was used here, and I think it helps convey the genuine atmosphere of the place. For the most part, men shuck oysters and women pick crabs. These women are mostly wives of watermen, and they are very adept at picking the meat out of the crabs. They know that the larger the lumps are, the more money it brings on the market.

51. Capt. Elliot's crab-picking operation, Grasonville, Maryland, July 28, 1993 MSA SC 1890-BP-26,828

Vietnamese and Cambodian women picking Chesapeake Bay crabmeat is a new twist because it used to be done by white and black housewives who were natives of the area. I've seen a lot of crab picking, but I've never seen it done more efficiently than these women were doing it. It was a very clean operation. They use a knife to pick the large lump crabmeat.

I took a pound of crabmeat home with me and I don't think I've ever had better. Of course, it was picked that morning and it was very fresh, but the lumps were large and that makes for better eating than the smaller pieces.

52. Capt. Bernard Hallock, Shady Side, Maryland, c. 1954

MSA SC 1890-MI-886A

I was doing a story on pound fishing back in 1954, and we went out with Captain Hallock. It was early morning. That's sunlight shining in his face, and you can see from the angle of the sun that it was very low in the sky. We went out right at sunup to run the nets. The sky forms a simple background because I was sitting down at a low angle, and I just sort of grabbed the picture.

He's not posing at all. He's just talking and probably was never aware the photograph was made. He's smiling, but not at me. He's obviously pleased with what he's saying.

53. Pound fishing, Shady Side, Maryland, c. 1954 MSA SC 1890-MI-1249A

Now, this is pound fishing, where fish have been brought in by the net, which is about a hundred yards long. The fish swim into a trap, and then the net is pulled up and the fish are dumped into the boats. These three men are going to start shoveling these fish into the boat, and then they'll pull the net up a little higher. You see the fish swirling around. I have no idea what kind of fish these are, but I remember they were sorting out the different types of fish when we brought them in. Trucks from Woodfield's were waiting for the fish to haul them down the road to Galesville to their packing house.

54. Shoveling menhaden from pound fisherman's boat, Wynne, Maryland, August 8, 1992 MSA SC 1890-BP-25,860

Menhaden are used for fish oil, chemicals, fertilizer, chicken feed, and bait. This is a small operation. When they are catching the menhaden for commercial purposes, they catch by the ton rather than by the little boatload like this. These will be used primarily for crab bait, either in crab pots or on trotlines. Some of it might wind up as commercial cat food.

54. Cat nipping, Wynne, Maryland, August 8, 1992 MSA SC 1890-BP-25,862

This cat had been going around from basket to basket trying to pick out a fish that it could have, or maybe one that smelled good. Here the cat is actually in the act of taking its fish. I turned the camera and quickly focused and grabbed the photograph. I think it tells the story quite well.

55. Cleaning rockfish, Deale, Maryland, April 20, 1991

MSA SC 1890-BP-24,964

For about eight years, they've had a moratorium on catching rockfish. Now you can catch them as a commercial or a sport fish, but they've got to be above a certain size and you have only a few days a year that you are able to go out.

This is at the end of a fishing tournament for rockfish down in Deale. I stopped by when they were weighing the fish and checking them in. Here they're cleaning and filleting them. When they cut up a fish, it's not very pretty and the action happens quickly.

I was shooting from a tripod, and I just barely got the man with "Mudds Liquor" on his T-shirt in the picture. I cut off the top of his head, but have the rest of his head and his eyes looking at what's going on. He's also holding a bottle of beer, which is quite natural, and I like the picture because it's very spontaneous, not posed at all. I included the absolute top of the negative in order to get this composition.

I crop pictures as little as possible, but once in a while you have to. The camera I'm using now, you either take horizontal or vertical, and so I have to make my decision when I take the photograph as to whether I want the end product as a vertical or a horizontal. When I was using a Hasselblad with a square format, I could make my decision later, and once in a while that worked to my advantage. But I usually take pride in making my decision when I take the picture.

56–57. Tug rendezvous, Patapsco River, 1968 MSA SC 1890-MI-2929 (35 mm)

Curtis Bay Towing Company used to have me cover the maiden voyage of every ship into Baltimore so that they could present the captain with a 16×20 print of their tugs assisting his ship. I'd get up at 3 A.M. and be out to the ship as she approached the harbor at sunrise. The most interesting time to cover the port is at dawn; the light is moody and there's always lots of action. This is probably the best photograph I ever made of a tugboat, but Curtis Bay never used it because it didn't show their vessels at work.

58. Freighter *Frances* passing beneath the Chesapeake Bay Bridge, 1960 MSA SC 1890-MI-14,533

My good wife and I had come across the Chesapeake Bay Bridge, and we saw this ship coming up the Bay, going toward Baltimore. I saw a truck sitting there, from the Chesapeake Bay Bridge Authority, and I pulled over and explained who I was and that I would like to go back out on the bridge and make a photograph of this ship going under. He said, "Sure, hop in the truck."

He drove out to the middle—now, this was when it was a two-lane bridge, by the way—and he put on his blinker lights. I saw where the ship was coming, and I saw the path of the sun on the water, and I said, "Ease along here," and then I said, "Now stop." I jumped out, and ran maybe ten feet in one direction or the other, and suddenly the ship was right where I wanted it to be. Looking down on the deck you see all of the rigging, so you know it's a freighter, it's not a passenger ship. It's done with 4 × 5, and so sharp that you can see every detail in it.

59. Longshoremen, Baltimore, Maryland, c. 1962

MSA SC 1890-MI-15,017-34 (35 mm)

I was the photographer for the Maryland Port Authority in its early days. The port was in bad repair then. They wanted to promote Baltimore in a good light, yet there was no attractive facility to show. I suggested that we emphasize the people. So this was one of a series of pictures that we titled "Building a Port."

These longshoremen were hired to unload ships. A crane brought the cargo over the side, and this was a safety net to save anything from falling into the water. The black areas of the photograph are open enough to see detail—and yet if you print it too light, it will look grey; if you print it too dark, it's just opaque. It's a delicate thing to print.

60–61. Whitehaven ferry, Wicomico River, June 12, 1986

MSA SC 1890-BP-20,957

When we go down to our daughter Nancy's, we usually go this way. It gets you off Route 50, and it also cuts about eight miles off our trip and is a very pleasant road.

The Whitehaven ferry is owned and operated by the State of Maryland. It is what

When we grew up, we didn't have anywhere to go, so we played in the skiffs, we played on the shores. We'd always go soft-crabbing when the season came. A lot of times we would wade. You'd have to be careful, though, because a lot of times you'd get your feet cut if you went barefooted because of the oyster shells that were on the bottom. Oysters were everywhere. And then the water was so beautiful. You could practically read a newspaper on the bottom. AUDREY ADAMS

they call a cable ferry. The ferry is brought across by this cable going through a series of pulleys. It only takes about two or three minutes for it to go across.

We went there one time when the water was too high for it to operate, so we went five miles to the upper ferry. We got across there, but it was rough.

The three-story building that you see there was an old hotel, and it's slowly deteriorating. There's been a big For Sale sign on it ever since we've seen it, but apparently nobody's interested in buying it. It would make a great bed and breakfast.

61. Ferry tender James Farington, Whitehaven Ferry, Wicomico County, Maryland, November 1990 MSA SC 1890-BP-24,443

There are two ferries, a few miles apart, across the Wicomico River below Salisbury. This is the one at Whitehaven. It can carry four cars; the other can carry two. They operate for free from sunup to sundown seven days a week, and you never have to wait more than five minutes to get on board. If they aren't running, you have to go to Salisbury to cross the river.

This man has been tending the ferry for years, and he was delighted when I asked to take his picture. He doesn't accept tips, but he often has fresh oysters or farm produce in baskets right there on the ferry. If you ask about them, he'll be glad to sell you some.

62. Night light, Shady Side, Maryland, c. 1954 MSA SC 1890-MI-1249B

I've always liked this picture. It was taken the first time I photographed pound fishing. At the end of the day, Raymond "Tuck" Fountain hung a lantern way out to indicate where the fishing nets were set so that boats could avoid them. The sign identified who owned the operation.

The starkness of the composition appeals to me. I also like the oversized kerosene container that assures that the beacon will shine all night and the oversized rubber overalls the man is wearing. It all seems very symbolic of the rough lives the watermen lead.

62–63. Crab scrape boat, Ewell, Maryland, July 1965

MSA SC 1890-SI-345 (35 mm)

This was shot with a 200 mm lens on 35 mm film, which foreshortens the image, isolates the subject from his surroundings, and adds impact. It really epitomizes the waterman going out to challenge the Bay, and it speaks to his lonely way of life. From this vantage point you see nothing but this one man and his boat; you can even see his muscles flexing as he's regulating the gas. There's a dustpan on the port side for bailing.

I've never printed this negative before; I guess it's because I took so many strong pictures on that first trip to Smith Island. Smith Island was entirely new to me then, and it was just so easy to see fresh angles. It's still that way on Smith Island. I guess when you get right down to it, I doubt I'll ever stop finding new perspectives on the Bay.

64–65. Crabber, Severn River, c. 1960 MSA SC 1890-MI-814

With a 4 × 5 camera you only get one chance at a shot like this. We'd been out on the Bay and were headed in at sunset when I saw this man crabbing from a flat-bottomed skiff at the mouth of the Severn River. The sun was just hitting his net and the reflections were perfect.

At the time I took the picture, I thought he was fishing. Twenty years later I went out crabbing with my son-in-law, who was using a technique I was unfamiliar with: running a trotline. When I learned the procedure—netting crabs along a line which bait is tied to—I suddenly realized that was what this man was doing when I made this picture.

I never tire of putting this negative in the enlarger and seeking out that quality print that's in my mind and that I know can be gotten from it. The most important aspect of printing is never being satisfied until you know you've gotten the best possible print. You can't watch the clock or worry about how much paper you're using. Sometimes, if you're in the right mood, you can get it absolutely right on the very first print, but that's rare. You've just got to discipline yourself to never be satisfied with anything short of the best possible print.

Land Labor

66. Trumpy's boatyard, Annapolis, Maryland, c. 1955 MSA SC 1890-MI-557A

Here are a carpenter and his helper fitting a plank around the ribs near the keel of a boat, and the recession of the lines gives it a very dramatic effect. When you frame something like this, you get this bull's-eye tunnel effect, and it adds a lot of drama to it. The man who's holding the board at the bow of the boat is wearing a hat and suspenders. That helps to date it because I don't think you'd see any workmen working on a boat today wearing a straw hat. The younger man has a cap on. That's more typical of today.

I used a tripod and a half-second exposure stopped down to twenty-two so I would have this depth of field. I had these guys hold this piece of planking up there while I made my shots.

68–69. Eastport, Annapolis, Maryland, c. 1960 MSA SC 1890-MI-1161-5

Trumpy's boatyard there in the center was a going affair building very large, very plush cabin cruisers for wealthy people. Trimmed with teakwood, each one of them was custom-made. Now this building out over the water has been converted into a restaurant and it's quite attractive, but anyone who goes in the restaurant would have no conception that large boats were built in there. The rest of the yard has been converted into smaller boat facilities or boat-oriented types of businesses.

Trumpy went out of business because they couldn't get the highly qualified carpenters that they needed to do this kind of excellent work, and a contributing factor was the building of the Calvert Cliffs nuclear plant down near Solomons. The gas and electric company was willing to pay much more per hour for a carpenter just to do construction-type carpentry than Trumpy could afford to pay to build a boat. But it was a dying industry anyway, because costs got so high for people to buy these boats and then maintain them. Only a few people wanted the luxury of teakwood, which requires a lot of maintenance, when you could buy a fiberglass boat that all you've got to do is hose it down.

70–71. Marina on Back Creek, Annapolis, Maryland, March 19, 1994

MSA SC 1890-BP-27,194

These days, most yachts are taken out of the water in the winter so they don't get damaged when the creeks freeze up. The hulls are set row upon row on blocks, with their masts forming a jungle. In the background you can see covered racks where smaller boats are stored.

This was taken on a sunny Saturday in March when I figured that people would be getting itchy to work on their boats. Sure enough, here was this man drilling something in the cockpit of his sailboat. There were a few other people around, but it was still pretty cold.

71. Willis Wilson, Deltaville, Virginia, March 29, 1993 MSA SC 1890-BP-26,460

Willis Wilson had this old engine going here on a marine railway, and he's pulling up a boat. He's watching the boat to see how far up the railway it is. The engine quit on him a number of times, and he had to get it restarted and then pull the boat up a little further, so he's very intent on what he is doing.

These caps, whether they're worn by a farmer or a waterman, are the uniform of the day. They never take them off. It starts as a boy. "Dad doesn't take his cap off, so I don't take my cap off."

You often go into a restaurant and see these guys eating their full meal with their caps on. There's very little difference between the caps that are worn by the farmers and the ones that are worn by the watermen. Most of them are advertising something, and they're all adjustable in the back so they fit everybody. Our son-in-law Charlie has twenty or thirty of these hats all hanging on the back porch, and if he wore one a day every day of the month, he couldn't wear the same one twice. He goes to these conventions, and they're handed out by the different feed producers.

72. Sail loft, Oxford, Maryland, April 17, 1968 MSA SC 1890-MI-2450B

I made this picture because it was a very colorful building. I like the word "Sailmaker" curved across Downes Curtis's name, and the clapboard siding on the building, and the way the wires come in. Up on the second floor, you see things stacked up in the window. There are two little black boys off in the distance playing in the yard.

Now the building has been covered with aluminum siding. I recently stood in the exact same spot and studied the building to see what other changes had been made. The steps were the same, the broken walk was the same, the shrubs had grown

High density of people does not lend itself well to the fisheries in general. I think that's been pointed out in all kinds of studies as to why we are having problems with grass growing on the bottom. Everyone wanted to point to toxic this and toxic that, and come to find out most of it was just soil, earth, dirt. Not so much what they were using but just the runoff from agriculture.

LARRY CHOWNING

considerably. The three fence posts that are visible here are still there, marking off a garden, and they're still exactly the same. Grass has grown where the roadway goes alongside the building, but the building that you see off on the righthand side behind is still there.

Today I would not set up the camera and take a picture of this building because with the modern aluminum siding on it, it doesn't have the character that it had before and yet it's exactly the same building.

73. Alfred and Downes Curtis, Oxford, Maryland, June 6, 1992

MSA SC 1890-BP-25,650

Downes Curtis's sail loft is actually an old schoolhouse. The second floor has a big expanse of hardwood floor, so he can lay his sails out and cut them.

He's got all kinds of job orders and notes and maps and calendars and tools and tape hanging on the wall. There's not an empty space on the wall, even around the shelving. He had no objection to being photographed, but he was a busy man and couldn't give us much time. He had a pencil alongside his glasses, which he would pull out frequently to mark something on the sail.

I supplemented this with flash, otherwise I would have had a very silhouetted photograph because I'm shooting directly out one of the windows. By using flash, I was able to balance the inside light, so you can still look outside and see the trees and the house next door. I dislike intensely to see a photograph like this where you see the direction of the flash; it has an artificial look about it. I purposely had the flash where the wrinkles in the sail showed, and yet I had good lighting on him.

I have other photographs with Downes more prominent, but this was a good one because it had his brother in it. Clearly Downes is in charge, because he's operating the sewing machine and Alfred is guiding the fabric. Many photographers ask for a subject to pose this way and to move their hand there. I simply waited until the hands were right and the sail showed right because the minute you tell them what to do, you've made it artificial, and it shows in their expression; it even shows in the way they hold their hands.

74–75. Edward Jones, Ewell, Maryland, March 12, 1991

MSA SC 1890-BP-24,741

Mr. Jones is a retired waterman who makes his living now by building replicas of all kinds of Chesapeake Bay workboats. He's painting a skipjack here, but he had bugeyes, buy boats, hand tong, and crab scrape boats, too. He's an excellent craftsman; I'd be proud to own one of his models.

I thought it would be too intrusive to bring a flash into his small shop, so I just used the natural light that came in through the windows and door. I picked my angle carefully to put the emphasis on him and the boats and, as a result, the boats hide some of the clutter. I left the broom leaning against the wall; it seemed like a nice touch, but I didn't want too many elements to distract your eye.

75. Ewell, Smith Island, Maryland, September 26, 1991

MSA SC 1890-BP-24,039

This is the kind of picture I dream about, finding people in animated conversation with dramatic lighting. I saw this old man talking to this woman, who was clutching her sack of groceries. She actually lives on Smith Island, but the man had gotten off a tour boat that had just landed. The women on the island seem to spend most of their time indoors—at least when I'm around—so I was delighted to catch this one on the road, and so, apparently, was this visitor.

76. I. P. Hudgins's store, New Point, Virginia, March 30, 1993

MSA SC 1890-BP-26,530

We went to New Point particularly to photograph the country store. We had been told that they had everything that pertained to the waterman and that they supply most of the wire and material to build crab pots in Maryland and Virginia and all over. Across the road was this big warehouse where all the raw material was stored, and I asked the man who worked there to roll out a bale of the wire. So this is a posed picture.

You can't use just plain chicken wire for crab pots. This wire is coated with corrosion-resistant paint, because the salt water would eat chicken wire up in less than a season if it weren't coated. Even when it is coated, when they bring the pots out of the water they have to dip them into tar. That makes them last another year or two.

That's one of the crabber's biggest expenses, replacing these pots, and they lose them both by rusting out and also by boats cutting the line or people stealing them. There's quite a high rate of casualties in crab pots.

77. Grey's store, Mason Springs, Maryland, May 1990 MSA SC 1890-BP-23,713

A few years ago, I had an assignment to photograph the Piscataway Indian community in Southern Maryland. I realized that the subjects I selected would leave a lasting impression of their culture, so I wanted to include a real cross-section of their activities. I asked whether there was a store owned and operated by Piscataways—I thought it was important to show entrepreneurship in the community.

Mr. Grey, his sister, and his wife run this grocery store in Mason Springs. It was a busy place when I arrived, so I roved around until they were finished taking care of their customers. By then I had selected this vantage point. I wanted to show these proud and prosperous storekeepers and to include as many of their products as possible. That way the portrait becomes a record of the general culture as well.

77. John Calabrese, Annapolis, Maryland, December 1990

MSA SC 1890-BP-24,583

For some years now, I've been trying to document various long-time businesses in Annapolis because I figure they won't be around too much longer. I walked by this barber shop on West Street almost every day, so I went in and asked Mr. Calabrese if I could make his portrait. Shortly after I made it, several people called me to tell me I'd better get in there soon and get his picture; he was closing his shop. But I'd already done it.

This picture was carefully thought out. I liked the decorations in the shop and wanted to include as much as possible. The picture over Mr. Calabrese's shoulder shows him as a much younger man and suggests the longevity of the business, and the framed certificate over the sink implies the pride he takes in his work. Obviously, the gallery of pictures on the opposite wall was an important part of the decor, so I caught them reflected in the mirror. Finally, I wanted the lighting to emphasize Mr. Calabrese rather than his customer, since he's the star of the show.

78. Detail, tobacco barn near Upper Marlboro, Maryland, c. 1988

MSA SC 1890-EP-7000

My first love is photographing people, but every once in a while I like to vary it a little bit and do a very careful study of patterns. This was done with a 4 × 5 camera. I studied everything in the ground glass for maybe fifteen or twenty minutes, planning what to include and what to exclude. I felt with the crosslighting that I really captured the texture.

78–79. Tobacco farm near Bay Ridge, Anne Arundel County, Maryland, c. 1956 MSA SC 1890-MI-14

For me, a photograph really succeeds if it can explain its subject completely. Here you can see the tobacco plant clearly in the foreground and that it is being harvested by hand and drawn by horses. There's the typical tobacco barn with its slats open for the crop to dry, and there's the farmer's house.

Today, of course, there would be a tractor out there instead of horses. In fact, this particular scene no longer exists; the community of Chrisland Cove on Bay Ridge Road is now on the site of this farm.

80–81. Soybean field, Somerset County, Maryland, c. 1987

MSA SC 1890-BP-7043

We were visiting our daughter Nancy on her farm, and I got up at sunrise and looked out the window and here was this soybean field with the mist on it and the light playing across it beautifully. So I very quietly got dressed and went downstairs to the car and got my 4 × 5 camera and my tripod and some holders, and came back up and went into the bathroom and closed the door and locked it. I took the screen off the window and set up the camera over the john because this gave me a good vantage point. I waited for the sun to get up a little bit, probably at least half an hour, and made the picture.

I made half a dozen exposures as the light changed and the fog lifted a little bit, and then when I got through, I folded up my equipment very quietly—because I thought everybody was sleeping—and opened the door, and there stood my son-in-law Charlie in his underwear saying, "What the hell are you doing in there? I've been waiting to get in there." Of course, there was another bathroom downstairs, but he'd been standing outside Lord knows how long, and he thinks I'm crazy anyway. It doesn't help one bit to have me crowding the bathroom at that hour of the morning, with a 4 × 5 camera, taking pictures of a soybean field.

But I liked the scene because not only do you have the soybeans in rows going away from the camera, but in the foreground is an end of the field in which you have a horizontal line plowed that holds the picture together very nicely. Fortunately, the early morning cloud bank adds a lot of interest to the sky.

One of the great satisfactions of taking pictures is doing a photograph like this that captures a feeling as well as a scene. I grew up in Missouri on a farm. My earliest recollections are of going out collecting the eggs and turning the cows out. As the sun was breaking, I often looked over the landscape and saw this particular scene of moisture rising off the green grass or green corn. I still get a great sensation out of getting up at dawn and seeing the sun come up, and the same thing with the sunset. I think sometimes sunrises are more interesting than sunsets because you have the moisture on the plants from the dew, and that adds a little more crispness to the photograph.

82. Plowed field in Charles County, Maryland, April 1991

MSA SC 1890-BP-23,581

I was down in the Piscataway Indian country, and as I drove down the road, I saw this plowed field with the sunlight giving beautiful texture to the furrows. There's a barn in the background, but as far as you can see, there's very roughly plowed land. I have no idea whether an Indian ever set foot on this particular plot of land, but I used it as a symbol of the Piscataways living in Southern Maryland.

This ground had been turned over for the winter. In the spring, they would come along with a harrow and run over this land to break up the clods and smooth it out, and then they'd come over it with a disk, which would break it down even further. Then this would become a very level field of just dirt. But in the fall, you do this to the land in order to fallow it for the winter, turning over the vegetation so it's buried and will rot and become fertilizer. This is the way we farmed when I was growing up, so this is what I assume was happening here.

83. Contour plowing, Clagett farm, Prince George's County, Maryland, October 1988 MSA SC 1890-BP-7260B

I like this because the big farmhouse is off in the distance, which gives you a scale to how large the farm is. This is a research farm owned by the Chesapeake Bay Foundation, and they do experimental plowing and harvesting and fertilizing.

Contour plowing is always done parallel to the roll of the land so that the water is held and does not run down a ditch. If it were plowed straight up the hill, the gullies would wash.

83. Ridge tillage, Clagett farm, Prince George's County, Maryland, November 20, 1987 MSA SC 1890-BP-22,361

One of the biggest problems you have in farming is topsoil runoff, because the minute you plow, you make the soil loose. When it rains hard, the soil can wash off into the streams and on down into the Bay, and it takes the nutrients off the land. This is an attempt at what they call ridge tillage, in which the dirt is plowed up and put into ridges about twelve, fifteen inches deep with gullies in between. Then the planter comes along and plants the seeds down in the ridge. The rain comes and wets the ridge, and the water runs into this gully, which is dead-ended. The water doesn't flow out; it just stands there and soaks the seed a lot longer as it seeps into the ground.

I've never seen this done except at this demonstration on the Clagett farm, though I understand that Chesapeake Wildlife Heritage uses it a lot on the Eastern Shore.

84. Loblolly pines near Taylor's Island, Maryland, 1968 MSA SC 1890-MI-2389

Snow pictures are very difficult to make because most of the time, particularly with naked trees in the wintertime, they look pretty barren. But here were these tall trees with the snow pressed against them, and snarly limbs all covered with snow, and there's a split tree and a separate tree that stand out, which gives it some composition and a point of impact.

A loblolly pine is used a great deal for fence posts. It's an indigenous tree to the Eastern Shore—in fact, all the way up and down the east coast to Georgia. It's a good tree because it grows thirty feet in the air without limbs on it, and without limbs, there are no knots. The trees that I've emphasized here are not loblollies. I don't have the remotest idea what they are, but you see the difference in the trees: these have limbs all the way down.

85. Near Taylor's Island, Maryland, 1968 MSA SC 1890-MI-2387-1

We had a tremendous snowstorm, and the next morning was bright and clear and cold, so I got in the car and took off for the Eastern Shore. I went on down the road toward Taylor's Island, and here was this field of corn stalks with a little barbed wire fence, and a house and barn off in the distance, and the snow blowing. I made the first

tracks in that snow. From a photographer's viewpoint, that's ideal because you don't have the imprint of somebody else.

It was probably below zero, or close to zero, because it was just bitter cold. It was one of those ideal days to do snow pictures because you had the crisp and blowing snow and bright sunshine. It's a rare thing in Maryland if you have those together. Usually you have a snow and it gets wet the next day and starts to thaw and melt. The minute it starts to melt, you lose the crispness of the snow.

It takes a lot out of you to be out in that kind of weather, all day long, photographing. Particularly with 4 × 5 equipment, because I didn't do these handheld; I did them with a heavy tripod. There was no way in that wind to hold a camera steady without a tripod.

86–87. Sunset near Lancaster, Pennsylvania, April 26, 1987

MSA SC 1890-BP-22,317

I was on an expedition to Amish country with some good friends. There were five of us photographers, the other four being amateurs I have worked with for many years. Everyone was very serious and really concentrating; it was quite an incentive to make good photographs. We were running up and down the road looking for a sunset photograph, when we saw this wonderful great big tree that had the limbs just so snarly that they formed a nice pattern of interest.

Over in the field was this young man plowing with a team of horses. We saw him going the other way, and we had to wait for him to go down and turn around. Well, he came back, and when he got up under the tree enough that he was part of the composition, I snapped the shutter. You can see the silhouette of the horses and of him holding the reins. They don't use mechanized equipment at all. They don't have electricity, they don't have power tools of any kind, and the plowing gets done by horses.

87. Barn raising, Intercourse, Pennsylvania, April 26, 1987

MSA SC 1890-BP-21,655

This wasn't the clearest afternoon, but you don't see an Amish barn raising everyday, so you make the best of what you have. There wasn't as much direction to the sun as I would have liked. I took a whole series of pictures, but I like this one, where the man has his hammer in midair, the best.

88–89. Amish farm, Paradise, Pennsylvania, April 26, 1987

MSA SC 1890-BP-21,704

The Amish use a lot of animal waste in their farming, and the runoff has an effect on the Bay's watershed. I like the way all the barns have silos in this photograph, and you can see several planes in recession.

90. Migrant workers near Pocomoke, Maryland, August 1990

MSA SC 1890-BP-6956

This was taken on a farm owned by a man named Veasey, who does truck farming. He raises tomatoes, peaches, and all kinds of crops. In fact, over on Route 13 he has a year-round stand in which he sells produce. There was only one man in this group of migrant workers who could speak English. He said they come up to work for Mr. Veasey in April and stay until October picking different crops, rotating from one crop to the other.

I did pictures of them picking in the field, but when they broke for lunch, I asked if they'd line up in a group. I don't often pose groups this way, but I thought this was kind of nice with the older men wearing hats. Migrant workers used to work in the oystering business and clamming, but most of those are gone now.

90–91. Migrant workers near Pocomoke, Maryland, August 1990

MSA SC 1890-BP-6949

These Mexican migrant workers were working on the Veasey farm down near Pocomoke City. I like this particular picture because we see three people in the foreground picking cucumbers. There's one man with an empty basket, another man with a full basket walking toward the truck, and a man at the truck handing up a basket of cucumbers.

Picking crops used to be done by tenant farmers on many of the big farms in this area, but now migrant laborers do most of that work.

I remember going to the picking houses with my mother. There wasn't any such thing as babysitters when we were growing up, and you weren't allowed to go in the factory. Your mother didn't have anything to do with you, so she had to take you with her. They'd go at like two and three o'clock in the morning, and we'd go to sleep in crab boxes. AUDREY ADAMS

92. Baling hay, Caroline County, Maryland, August 30, 1988
MSA SC 1890-BP-22,024

When I came down this little country road and saw these people baling hay, I got out and started making photographs. This was made with a fairly long lens so that I wouldn't be out in the field where they would stop or would be watching me out of the corner of their eye. Everybody's quite natural.

Having done this as a boy growing up on the farm, I knew exactly when the action would be right. When I got there they had almost a full load of hay. I let them go back and forth through the hayfield a few times, and then they got rid of that wagon and came back with another. But I didn't want an empty wagon, so I waited until they had enough hay on the wagon to show what was happening.

The other very important thing here is that you have a typical farmhouse of the Eastern Shore, a few outbuildings, a silo, a barn, and even a tree with an old tire swing hanging in the yard. All these things are so typical of farm life. You feel that you have a little idea of the farm, and farm life, and the people who work there from a picture like this.

Fortunately, the three boys on the wagon were all wearing white shirts, which helps to give strength to the photograph, and the guy driving the tractor is wearing a white cap; all that adds to the impact of the photograph.

93. Courthouse Hill Road, Somerset County, Maryland, February 10, 1986 MSA SC 1890-BP-20,515

Spontaneous as it may look, I waited fifteen or twenty minutes to make this photograph. There is a cedar tree on one side of this lonely country road, and the utility poles are lined up on the other side. It's a hazy Eastern Shore day. The scene seemed to symbolize country living on the Shore, but the composition needed something more. When I thought about it, I realized that the really typical thing is some guy—or a woman, either one—driving along in a pickup truck. It seems like there are ten pickups for every car. I photographed three different trucks, but this is the one I liked best. I waited until I could see the driver silhouetted through the windshield.

94. Produce stand near Salisbury, Maryland, September 1, 1988
MSA SC 1890-BP-22,090

Along the roads, particularly on the Eastern Shore, you have all of these produce stands empty and boarded up in the wintertime, and then as produce starts to come in, they open up and develop more and more signs stretched up the road. Some of these stands are very ordinary and have no appeal to them, but this one was, I thought, kind of nice. You've got Lopes—cantaloupes—with the O shaped like a cantaloupe, and hot dogs, and Silver Queen corn. The signs seem to work, because this stand was well attended.

94. Farmers market, Annapolis, Maryland, July 1990 MSA SC 1890-BP-24,172

This picture was made out at the Anne Arundel County Farmers Market on Riva Road, and it shows people buying produce from the farmers—cabbages in the foreground, cucumbers, green peppers, and squash. It's a good picture of people interacting.

I was set up there for probably ten minutes, and at first the people at the booth began to watch me, but then after I sat there a few minutes and maybe even made an exposure or two, why, their interest went back to selling produce.

This is a case where I filled with flash, and yet even the flash out there in the daylight didn't seem to bother anybody. Once it goes off, it's too late for them to pose, except that they are aware of you for the next photograph. But if you are patient, you can outwait them.

This is an entirely different approach to the same subject as the picture of the woman selling produce on the side of the road (on page 95). In this case, I've got the public involved. In the woman's case, I'm the public. She's offering all this to the camera, where here they're not even aware of the camera.

95. Selling vegetables, West Point, Virginia, April 5, 1990
MSA SC 1890-BP-23,960

I bought some onions from this woman. I was drawn by her pleasant attitude and her naturalness. She seemed like a do-it-yourself type of person, there all by herself, pulled off to the side of the road in the middle of nowhere.

When I took her picture, I wanted to be sure to include all the elements of the scene: the back of her truck, the folding table, the scale where she weighed her produce, the prices clipped to the boxes, the plastic bag in her hands. Fortunately, the light was at the right angle so that it played off the vegetables to make them really appealing.

96–97. Cokesbury Road, Somerset County, Maryland, August 5, 1985 MSA SC 1890-BP-22,005

I spent a good bit of time on Cokesbury Road because that's where my daughter Nancy lives. This day I was going up the road and I saw the mailman putting mail in this box. I said to myself, "When I lived in the country, I always watched for the mailman. When he came, I went right out and got my mail." So I pulled off at the next driveway and got out my camera with a long lens and waited. Sure enough, I hadn't been there three minutes when this woman walked out and opened the box.

Without the woman, this would be a pretty dull picture. But as it is, with the big shade tree and the wire from the utility pole headed off in that direction, you know that there's a residence there without even seeing it.

Looking Upstream

98. Cumberland Narrows, Allegany County, Maryland, October 1958 MSA SC 1890-MI-1195

When I took this picture of the Cumberland Narrows back in 1958, the Chesapeake Bay was the farthest thing from my mind. I was taking a picture of the mountains and the Potomac River in the valley, not the watershed of the Bay. Now I realize that it's a strong symbolic image for the theme of looking upstream.

I've always told my wife that this is my favorite portrait of her. We were on a trip celebrating our fifteenth wedding anniversary.

To set up this shot, Mary and I were able to drive only part way up the mountain to a deserted nightclub. From there we had to carry all of the heavy and cumbersome 4 × 5 camera equipment up the hill. Then Mary continued to climb out to the promontory called Lover's Leap. I told her I wanted an action shot, but she wouldn't go along with it.

100–101. Georgetown, Maryland, on the Sassafras River, September 9, 1958 MSA SC 1890-MI-1741

I think this shot symbolizes the Eastern Shore landscape. I like the way it shows the lay of the land with the Sassafras River snaking through it in such an interesting pattern. Dave Scott, my pilot, was a sailor; he was the one who first noticed this view of Georgetown. I'm sure it was the sailboats that caught his eye. He loved photography as much as I do and was always helping me find a good subject.

102. Allen's Fresh, Maryland, August 7, 1992 MSA SC 1890-BP-6986A

Allen's Fresh is on the Wicomico River on the Western Shore of Maryland, and it drains into the Potomac. Few people know that there are two Wicomico Rivers in Maryland and two more in Virginia. This river only runs for a few miles, so it isn't anywhere near as well known as the Wicomico on the Eastern Shore. Its headwaters are actually well above Allen's Fresh, at the source of the Zekiah Swamp.

This, I think, is a very fine example of tidal wetlands. The tide comes up over this land and pretty well submerges a lot of the grasses; when it goes down, they dry out. Here the tide is out because you see a lot of the mud. This is a great habitat for shedding crabs and waterfowl.

I made a picture of Allen's Fresh in color probably twenty years ago, which I have sold a number of times as a particularly good wetlands panorama of the Chesapeake Bay. I did it in the spring when the grasses were very, very green and the sky was very blue. It was dramatic; but for this project in black and white, I wanted to go back and do it over again. I had planned to do it in the afternoon, when the sun was on the far side of it, so that I'd have a little backlighting, which makes everything stand out. Fortunately, I had a few clouds, and I also had the reflection of the clouds, which helps a lot. There were egrets and herons, but they were quite small off in the distance.

103. Warren's Ferry, Virginia, July 14, 1993 MSA SC 1890-BP-26,771

Warren's Ferry is down from Charlottesville a few miles. Across the James River, we see the slope of the land where the ferry landing used to be. There's a big cable around a sycamore tree that's remaining—the cable is from the time of the ferry.

Two fishermen are coming in to meet their families. The children were playing and swimming in the river. There's a lot of industry farther up the James, so there may be serious contamination coming from there.

The theory used to be: any toxic that you put in the water is dissolved and disappears a mile downstream. When I was a kid, our septic tank dumped into a river. We

Up these rivers, what you end up with is winding channels, deep water, fifty, sixty, seventy feet in some cases, big meander turns that have got cut banks, in some cases high bluffs on the outsides of the turns, great big marshes on the insides, huge expanses of real high-quality, freshwater, annual seed-bearing plants—wild rice, pickerelweed, arrow arum, smartweed, tearthumb—big, heavy seed producers, real good habitat, real good food for waterfowl. They grow a lot of catfish and eels and mud shad, which are favorite foods for the national bird. This is where most of the Bay's eagles are, up in the rivers. JOHN PAGE WILLIAMS

thought that a mile downstream it was all clear again. You could swim there or do anything you wanted. Well, of course, now we know that's not so.

103. Fishing on the Rivanna River, Columbia, Virginia, July 14, 1993 MSA SC 1890-BP-26,731

This is one of those lucky breaks in photography. We were exploring up the James River, and we drove down on a point of land and stopped. Turns out we were at the confluence of the James and Rivanna Rivers, but we didn't realize it at the time.

Mame called me and said, "Here comes this boat up the river—people fishing." I ran with my camera and got there in time to get them as they were casting up the river. The trees make it a very well-framed and attractive shot. The sunlight, fortunately, was coming out just soft enough to give me light direction and a nice reflection in the water.

To get this photograph, I had to scramble down a rather steep bank, and I caught myself on a tree. My philosophy is to scramble to the point where you can get the photograph and take the risk if necessary. If I had hesitated and said, "Oh, I can't get down there," or "Here, give me a hand," I wouldn't have made that picture; it would have been too late. Had I slipped, I would have fallen right in the river, but that's part of the risk you take.

104–105. Gray's Creek, near Scotland, Virginia, July 30, 1993
MSA SC 1890-BP-26,870

This is where we started our trip down the James River to Norfolk. It's a little creek that goes about a mile up off the James. I got two of my best pictures when we started the trip—one looking upstream and one looking downstream.

Here I'm on a bluff of thirty feet, maybe, looking upstream. I'm up another ten or twelve feet on top of my van, which lets me look over the trees and frame the view upstream. The view downstream showed more grass.

If I'd stayed on the ground, this tree that's centered in the foreground would have blocked much of the view, particularly the boathouse on up the creek. So by getting up high, I was able to look down on the creek a bit more. The dead stump of a tree that's remained there probably for many, many years suggests the cycle of plant life that happens naturally up and down a creek.

106–107. Wenona, Maryland, 1990 MSA SC 1890-BP-7302A

When I first saw these boats up this stream in the marshes, all of them abandoned, I thought it would make a great photograph, but it was the wrong time of day. Some time later, we were down spending the weekend with our daughter Nancy, and Wenona is about fifteen miles from her house, so I said, "Let's go over there." I thought that about ten o'clock in the morning the light would start to fall on the planked side of this derelict boat. So I got there about ten o'clock, and lo and behold, it was totally in shadow.

Well, it turned out that it took about an hour and a half for the sun to move over enough so that I got sunlight on the planking. Sunlight adds emphasis and good lighting on these other boats, too. You see a lonely tree, then a couple more over on the left, and a vast area of wetlands and water beyond. These derelict boats are all just abandoned, and it makes quite a statement about what happens to boats. When the tide comes in, they probably float some, and then when the tide goes out, they sink down in the mud; and between the summer and high tides and the winter and all, they just come apart.

This is a very primitive thing that people do where there's space to do it. I can remember growing up on the farm, if we had a piece of farm equipment that we no longer used or hadn't any plans to use immediately, we abandoned it in the yard, and pretty soon another piece got there, and it wasn't too long before we had the place cluttered with farm equipment. These things can't happen in urban areas because of the closeness of living. But here in this raw countryside where everybody does it, they think nothing of it. It's a sign of rural living, and the fact that it isn't crowded, and that all the laws of civilization haven't taken effect.

107. Abandoned skipjack, Knapps Narrows, Maryland, August 29, 1992 MSA SC 1890-BP-25,983

This picture conveys the passing of the era of the skipjack. You see the rudder and the deckhouse and the wheel of the boat, and anybody who has ever seen a skipjack, or who knows anything about them, is immediately going to identify this as a picture of a skipjack and not any other boat on the Bay. The skipjack is the symbol of watermen and the Chesapeake Bay.

I don't like contrived photographs. Here I didn't touch a thing; all I did was pick the angle I wanted and the height. Fortunately, the sunlight was quite good on it. I would like to have been an hour earlier so I'd have had a little crosslighting on the deckhouse, but on the other hand, the rough paint does show up quite well. The thing I really liked was that there are some weeds growing up on the deck, which just shows how long the boat's been tied up there. Enough dirt has settled in and enough seeds have fallen there to produce a two-foot plant.

107. Derelict bugeye, Mill Creek, near Solomons, Maryland, August 7, 1991 MSA SC 1890-BP-25,210

One of the things that I find intriguing is what happens to these old wooden boats. Everything is becoming fiberglass, and these old wooden boats are disappearing. A friend of mine took me up Mill Creek in his runabout to show me this boat. It was just about to split in half; the bow, the stern, and the mid-section were all under water.

That's one of the nice things about getting local people to take me out. They know where things are. There's no way in the world I would ever have found this boat by myself. Later I learned from Fred Hecklinger that she was a motorized bugeye once owned by Preston Lore, who used to use her for dredging.

108–109. New Windsor, Carroll County, Maryland, October 26, 1992 MSA SC 1890-BP-25,451

I thought this made a very dramatic photograph showing the tillage of the land, a nice farmhouse with a brick-end barn, and other farms off in the distance. Then way off, you begin to pick up the mountains, which eventually lead to the end of the watershed. On this side of the Alleghenies, the water will flow toward the Chesapeake Bay, and on the other side, the chances are it flows into the Ohio River. The contour plowing here in this slightly rolling countryside is the way they're protecting the soil from erosion.

109. Amish school house, Intercourse, Pennsylvania, April 26, 1987
MSA SC 1890-BP-21,686

This is a little Amish school built of white stucco, and there's an Amish man in his hat and vest, the typical uniform of the Amish men, standing on the front porch. The doors are open, and I presume school was going on. Through the trees you can see the school steeple with a bell in it. It just makes a nice picture.

110. Susquehanna River near Towanda, Pennsylvania, c. 1989
MSA SC 1890-BP-22,931

This is probably the farthest away from the Chesapeake Bay that I've taken a picture to show its watershed. This is way up the Susquehanna River in Pennsylvania. It was taken from a bluff, looking up the river toward a couple of islands and the rolling hills. Actually, this river is 440 miles long and goes all the way to Cooperstown, New York, where it is just a little stream.

People who live up here probably don't even think about the fact that if they put a tin can, or a beer can, in the water, it may eventually wind up in the Chesapeake Bay. But it's entirely possible that it will, along with other pollutants that are far less visible.

111. Confluence of the James and Rivanna Rivers, Columbia, Virginia, July 15, 1993 MSA SC 1890-BP-7020

Few people ever see the confluence of two rivers. This is a vantage point Mame and I found one evening too late to make the photograph. The next day we came all the way back from Richmond especially to make this photograph in late afternoon. We arrived about three, four o'clock in the afternoon, and already the sun was pretty much off the scene. That doesn't really bother me because the photograph has detail in the bank and on the trees and up the rivers. I made this with my 4 × 5 camera up on a bridge that crosses the James River at Columbia.

111. Potomac River at Great Falls, Maryland, October 2, 1989
MSA SC 1890-BP-22,989

Great Falls is a difficult place to photograph because really all you get, in most cases, is just a few rocks with a lot of water rushing over them. Being at the fall line of the Potomac River makes it a very important site. You can bring ships in a river up to the fall line, and at the fall line, there's usually a good drop from one height to another. This is probably the most dramatic fall line of any of the rivers in the Chesapeake Bay region, and probably one of the best known.

I lived in Crisfield when my children were going to high school. I enjoyed it in the winter, but when spring would come, I'd get a yearning to come home. My mother-in-law went to visit her daughter up in Baltimore one year, and she said she was all right as long as she was housed in and couldn't go out. But when spring come, she said, "I long to get home and bury my heels in the mud!"

VIRGINIA EVANS

It's a very popular place with painters. This young lady is crouched down on one of these rocks very precariously, with her easel, painting the scene. She gives a little human interest and scale to the photograph.

Great Falls is an important recreation area because of the scenery and the rapids. It's also a very dangerous place because people try to swim in it, and there are great eddies and backwaters that suck people down. It's treacherous, too, because it's calm in drought periods and the water flows and falls very gently, but if a rain comes upstream, water comes rushing down and swells over the rocks. I've heard of people being stranded because they're sitting out on the rocks, thinking they can wade back onto shore very easily; but because it rained upstream, here comes this gush of water down, and they have to be rescued.

112–113. Reserve fleet, James River, July 30, 1993 MSA SC 1890-BP-26,908

This is a reserve fleet of merchant ships and navy ships up the James River. I tried to take a photograph that had impact and also showed more than one grouping of ships. They were grouped half a mile apart, which made them hard to relate to one another. If you look closely, you'll see the corner of one group in the foreground and then two groups tied off side by side. Between the two groups you see a third group off in the distance. This photograph is highlighted by an ordinary powerboat, a fishing boat that is very hard to see because of the tremendous size of these ships, passing through the water to the left.

The main channel goes between two of these tied-up, anchored fleets. We counted close to two hundred ships just rusting away. A lot of them are repairable, and during the Iraqi conflict a couple of years ago, some of them were called back into service to haul things to the fleet. So they do serve a purpose, but there's no sense in keeping them tied up at a dock where it's expensive.

It's kind of ghostly here: you feel these are ships of the past. They are enormous, and to see so many of them tied up together is impressive.

114–115. Fishing on the shore of the Susquehanna River near the spillway of Conowingo Dam, September 3, 1986 MSA SC 1890-BP-21,220

This was taken from up on Conowingo Dam looking downstream. You see people way off in the distance, silhouetted, fishing on the rocks. It's quite different from what you'd see on the Potomac River or on the James, where the rivers are much wider.

115. Jug Bay, Prince George's County, Maryland, August 24, 1986
MSA SC 1890-BP-7350

On the Prince George's side of Jug Bay, they have built a lot of walkways to let you go out and experience the wetlands, but this is a pier that was out there expressly for fishing. Fortunately, I got a guy who has just caught a fish. That's one of the more difficult things to do when you're out taking fishing pictures. Fishermen don't just pull them in one after another. And usually when they do catch one, they pop it out of the water real quick because they don't want it to get off the hook. You've got to be fast to catch them with the pole bent and a fish on the hook. So I feel fairly fortunate to have this.

The land that you see beyond the pier is a fine example of wetlands, and it extends for a great distance. But the impressive thing is that all this part of the Patuxent River was navigable a hundred years ago, and now most of it is very shallow water. The land was cleared of timber, then it was plowed every year and the rains washed the soil down into the little streams. The streams took it out into the river, and the river filled up with silt. Then grasses started to grow. As a result, a great expanse of wetland was created, but the navigable waters were lost. Lord knows what would have happened had this land not been developed; the water would probably have stayed deep.

This will eventually be solid ground if it continues the way it is. The grasses will stop additional silt from going down the river, and the more they stop, the more muddy the wetland becomes. Eventually it becomes solid ground, and then pretty soon a tree sprouts out on it. It's a continually changing situation.

115. St. Ignatius cemetery on the Potomac River near Piscataway, Maryland, April 19, 1990 MSA SC 1890-BP-23,528

This picture was made as part of my Piscataway Indian project. When people told me that all the Indians were buried down at St. Ignatius Church on the Potomac River, I said, "Well, you know, that's something I'd like to get." Most of the Indians are buried way down the hill, and there are not very many marked graves. But up here on top, I spotted this. It says Piscataway Indian, Madeline Swann Robinson. By this time, I knew that Robinson and Swann were common names among the Piscataway Indians, but I don't even have to identify in a caption that she was a Piscataway. It says so right there.

Home Ports

116. City Dock, Annapolis, Maryland, c. 1963 MSA SC 1890-MI-531

I was struck by this scene at City Dock as soon as I saw it. The *Anna Florence* was an old motorized bugeye being used as a buy boat. I learned recently that the deck house is now the ticket office at the maritime museum in St. Michaels.

118–119. Sunrise on Spa Creek, Annapolis, Maryland, July 5, 1993
MSA SC 1890-BP-26,686

This is another one of those pictures you see ahead of time and then go back and do. My wife and I had walked down to the water at the end of Southgate Avenue, and when I looked down Spa Creek I could see that this would be a good early morning picture. So a morning or two later, I got in the car and went over there, and sure enough, here came the sun up right behind St. Mary's Church. When it got up high enough to cast a good reflection on the water, I took the picture.

The photograph shows a number of boats anchored in kind of a misty haze, with the good reflections that you usually get in the early morning before the wind has come up. The sun gives it a highlight. Without the sun, it would have been a very dull photograph.

I don't think you ever wear out the ability to find a new angle on things. I've photographed Spa Creek many times. Five years ago, I did a picture looking out Old Woman Cove from Lafayette Avenue (on page 180), a few blocks away from this scene. They're on the same creek, but you look at the two photographs and you'd never realize they were taken anywhere near each other because the lighting and the atmosphere are totally different.

120. Morning boat from Smith Island to Crisfield, Maryland, November 11, 1992 MSA SC 1890-BP-26,284

This is a picture that I have been trying for every time I've gone to Smith Island. It's a difficult photograph to make because you're in a moving boat, inside where people are, and usually the boat is going at a pretty good clip. The problem was that either it was very, very crowded or there were very few people on the boat. Here, on a Wednesday morning, were a number of the ladies from Smith Island going in to shop at Crisfield. This is not recreation; it's their only way to do any real shopping. And they have to take this boat in to Crisfield to do it.

120–121. Ewell, Smith Island, Maryland, September 25, 1967
MSA SC 1890-MI-2290-3

This is an aerial of the town of Ewell on Smith Island. Way off in the distance, the little speck you see with houses on it is Tylerton. There's also a town named Rhodes Point, off to the right on down the road, that does not appear in this photograph.

There have been a lot of changes from the mid-sixties when this picture was made. The watermen used to go out in skiffs to these floater boxes—those little squares that are enclosed in the large rectangles—and take out the soft crabs. All of those shedding boxes are now up on dry land in sheds, and it's a much more efficient way of tending to the peelers.

Some of the structures near the rectangles are still there as wrecks, just out in the water, falling apart; but most of them are gone, totally gone. Probably every house that you see in this picture is still there today, plus a few more. The grammar school is the same, the ball field, and, of course, the church.

There are actually three ways to get to Smith Island by boat. The most popular way is from Crisfield, about twelve miles away. But there is also an excursion boat that comes from Virginia, down near Reedville, and the Smithsonian brings groups from Point Lookout to Smith Island.

Smith Island is really a group of islands. It used to be all one island, but the land has slowly settled down to where now you can't go from one place to the other except by water. As a matter of fact, there's very little solid ground. Where the trees are is the only high land, and that's only about two to three feet above sea level. The water is encroaching more and more onto Smith Island, and they predict that in not too many years they may have to abandon the island, as other islands on the Bay have been abandoned in years past.

The Smith Island diet is amazing. Have you ever heard of Jimmy crabs and dumplings? It's amazing. They take Jimmy crabs, they take the back off, clean them, and scrub them all around the shell and the claws and everything. And then they stew them and put some turnips and potatoes and big dumplings, so it's like this real viscous stew kind of thing with these crabs with their accoutrements still intact. You've got to go in there with a fork and a knife and pick the crab in the stew.

REUBEN BECKER

122–123. Marsh at Ewell, Maryland, November 8, 1992

MSA SC 1890-BP-26,181

This shows the proximity of man and nature on Smith Island, how close he lives to the water. Everybody has waterfront property, so to speak. The grasses help to prevent erosion. If it weren't for these grasses, the island would be long gone. The wave action is stopped by the grasses, and it takes wave action to erode the land away. Now, that doesn't mean that a storm can't come in and take some of the land. That happens all the time.

123. Smith Island, Maryland, July 1965 MSA SC 1890-SI-74 (35 mm)

These children playing on their tricycle and toy car give scale to the narrow streets on Smith Island. These boys have long since grown up and may well be among the watermen I've photographed in recent years on the island. The mailboxes now have enormous street numbers on them to comply with the county's emergency 911 system.

123. Elliott, Maryland, March 4, 1986 MSA SC 1890-BP-20,595

Elliott, Maryland, is the end of the earth. You go down to Vienna, and instead of staying on Route 50 across the bridge toward Salisbury, you take a sharp right turn and go through the town of Vienna and down a little country road. The road narrows to one lane; it only goes to Elliott.

The first time I went there I was with Mary, and we had no idea what was at Elliott. We just saw on the map that there was a little point at the end of the road. We kept going and going and going, and finally we came to this little village. There were two churches and about ten houses and a cemetery, and that was it.

As we were turning around to come back, a storm was blowing up and a great black cloud came up behind this pure white church and cemetery. There are dozens and dozens of churches like this on the Eastern Shore, white churches with a steeple and pointed windows, and they get to look pretty much alike. But this particular church with that storm behind it stood out. The storefront there with a canopy, and the houses beyond, and the cemetery up in front seemed to just say the village church a little differently.

It pays to go back to these communities at different times of the day and at different seasons. This is a sort of hunt-and-peck method of taking photographs, but I don't know any other way to do it. There's no way to say, "I'm going to Elliott today and make a fine picture," because you don't know if it's going to be there. Sometimes you go down these roads and don't even open a camera.

124. Cokesbury Road near Pocomoke, Maryland, April 1, 1991

MSA SC 1890-BP-24,854

We say the camera doesn't lie, but you can make it say most anything you want. I'm very guilty of it, trying to make a statement about the changes in the Bay region. If I were a developer, I would probably be showing all the modern things and all the modern houses. But here I am trying to capture the era that's now passing. The purpose in doing this whole project is to document this period of time. You have the feeling that when a modern house is built, it's going to be there for a long time, so you don't need to take a photograph. But an older house, you feel, "That may go." "That may not be here next year." And so often it is true. So my camera is far more inclined to photograph what is endangered than what has just been built and is potentially going to be there for a long time.

This is a house on Cokesbury Road near my daughter Nancy's house in Somerset County. I've studied this house for years, actually, because I like the style of it, and I like the way it's set up on this little rise and has the trees around it. It looked to me like a very typical farmhouse with its outbuildings and I wanted to make a photograph of it, but the light was never the way I wanted it: either it wasn't clear enough or was coming from the wrong direction.

This particular day I was driving along and I said, "Oops, there it is." I pulled off the road and got my tripod out and set it up and made this photograph, and it was just exactly what I had visualized. It's early enough in the spring that the trees other than the evergreens haven't leafed out yet. In mid-summer the trees are so heavy you don't get this sort of isolated feeling about it that shows here.

124. Virginia Route 695 near Saxis, Virginia, August 28, 1989

MSA SC 1890-BP-22,919

I passed these people as I drove toward Saxis, so on the way back I stopped and asked them if I could take their picture. Nobody moved. I thought it was pretty amazing to have a perfect stranger pull up to a scene like this and take out a camera and have nobody move an inch. When I drove by a few weeks later, they were still there.

I took this group from two angles. One was almost straight on, but I prefer this one where the vantage point adds emphasis to the composition. I like the man's relaxed hands hanging over the railing. I used a flash to fill in the shadows under the porch; otherwise there would be very little detail.

125. Home port, Elliott, Maryland, March 4, 1986 MSA SC 1890-BP-20,592

Finding people when you're taking photographs like this just seems to be impossible. They're either inside doing something or they're out on the water, so you have to settle for a document of how they live. Particularly in the rural areas of the Eastern Shore, there's a great deal of similarity to the style of frame houses and almost no brick houses at all.

This is a typical Eastern Shore house, with brown asbestos shingle siding and a brown asphalt shingle roof. In the front yard, propped up on wooden blocks, is a workboat built on the Hooper's Island model. It's being painted; nobody's working on it, but you can see the strokes of the paint and the fact that the water line has not been cut in yet.

This is a scene that you see fairly often on the Eastern Shore. I thought this one was particularly good because the front door shows quite well in the picture, and a couple of snarly trees help to show that it is an old, established area, not a new development.

Even the double chimney on the left side of the house and the cinderblock chimney alongside the original chimney tell you something. There's obviously another form of heat, or another stove was put in at some later date.

When I'm traveling on the road, my eyes are always looking to the right or left to see scenes like this. Here all the elements really tied together to pick up the statement that I was trying to make about a waterman's house and his boat in the front yard.

126–127. Arundel on the Bay, Fishing Creek, and Thomas Point, Maryland, May 8, 1970 MSA SC 1890-MI-2720-7

I took this aerial a long time ago, probably just as a nice pattern shot of the distinctive shape of the Thomas Point peninsula and the light reflecting on Fishing Creek. That's a Coast Guard station on the creek in the lower foreground, and Thomas Point light is just out of the range of my camera.

Today the picture has added significance because much of this land now has housing on it. There are both tidal and nontidal wetlands in this view, and I often wonder how it happened that houses could be built in such an environmentally sensitive area. I guess the property was just too valuable to leave undeveloped.

128. Nassawadox, Virginia, June 29, 1989 MSA SC 1890-BP-7259

I stopped to make this picture because it had two of the elements of a very small town: the railroad crossing and the three country stores. This was taken with a 4 × 5 camera and very carefully composed to include just these elements.

Nassawadox is right on Route 13 on the Eastern Shore of Virginia. You see very few people. I was there probably half an hour making this picture and literally nobody showed up, and it was the middle of the afternoon. I like people in photographs, but so often you find a subject like this and can't round up people to be in it. I don't mean I want to pose people; I want them there naturally. Sometimes I'll wait half an hour or longer for someone to pull in, go in and get the mail, or walk out with some groceries. It just didn't happen on this particular occasion.

I think these buildings have character, all the way down to the For Sale signs in the window. This shows a passing era because once these merchants give up their businesses, chances are the stores will just be boarded up. People now go ten or twenty, thirty miles down the road to the shopping center instead of patronizing these places. It's amazing how many of these individually owned stores have disappeared in the short period of time that I have been documenting them.

129. St. Michaels, Maryland, September 25, 1986 MSA SC 1890-BP-21,344

In many towns, buildings are sort of nondescript and not very photogenic. But here I was able to get the Main Street of St. Michaels framed with a tree in the foreground and a church at the other end, and with the town hall visible, as well as stores. Fortunately, I got people walking on the street and a couple of people sitting on a bench. The scene is nicely crosslighted.

When I first saw St. Michaels, it was a pretty quiet town, but later it was one of the first communities, even ahead of Annapolis, to become very tourist oriented. Now the stores carry sports items and novelties that are not typical of the small rural towns that only serve the natives and farmers nearby.

230

Back in them days, my wife, she'd get up, even if I got up at three o'clock in the morning, and get my breakfast and get my lunch to carry with me during the day. And when I come home, she'd always have my meal ready for me. EDWARD HARRISON

The Chesapeake Bay Maritime Museum is there, which is a big attraction. Along with that came the Crab Claw and other good restaurants. Also, it's a very wealthy area because people from Delaware retire there since there's a lot of good waterfront property and the Miles River is a very fine harbor for sailing. St. Michaels is the principal port of log canoe racing. Oxford would probably argue that point, but the two towns are not that far apart.

129. Card players, Bloxom, Virginia, June 29, 1989 MSA SC 1890-BP-22,837

I was wandering around Bloxom one day when I saw a Pool Hall sign and looked in the open door. These men were playing cards in the back, so I went in and introduced myself and asked whether I could take their picture. The owner said no. I continued to watch them for a while, then got up to leave. As I said goodbye, I told them I thought they'd be a great addition to my Bay Project photographs, and one of the players said, "Oh, why don't you let him do it?" So the owner said it was okay, and I went and got my camera. I set it up on the tripod and just continued to watch until they forgot I was there.

The next time I was by Bloxom, I took several prints to the owner for him to give to all the guys.

130–131. Grandparents' day at school, Tylerton, Maryland, September 26, 1991 MSA SC 1890-BP-24,089

I understand that this is the only one-room grammar school in operation in the state of Maryland. I think it's exaggerating to say it's a one-room school because there are a number of rooms, but there's only one big classroom.

It's grandparents' day, and the grandparents were all invited to come. The children performed for them, and afterwards they had cake and soda pop. I talked to a camera group over at Princess Anne recently, and when I walked into the classroom it looked exactly like this. Even though this is the one-room school in Tylerton, it is probably typical of a grammar school classroom anywhere.

131. Schoolhouse, Warsaw, Virginia, August 7, 1986 MSA SC 1890-BP-7045C

I went down to the Northern Neck of Virginia on a field trip sponsored by the Chesapeake Bay Foundation. As we were coming back in the afternoon, nearly finished with the trip, we were on roads I'd never traveled before. I looked out the window and saw this wonderful old schoolhouse with the light coming right on it. I made a little note of every time we turned so I could come back to it. After we got to our cars, I went backwards over my notes and got right back to this wonderful little schoolhouse. It was abandoned and the clapboards were coming off, but it had this distinctive little cupola on it.

The steps were all overgrown with weeds, and I went ahead and made a picture just as I found it. Then I took my machete and cut down some of the weeds, and I made another picture, and then I went back and cut down more of the weeds so that you could see the actual steps into the school and the bottom of the clapboard. The fact that it doesn't have a basement—that the building is sitting on blocks—seemed to be important to me, but at the corners and around the back, I didn't cut down the undergrowth. I could decide later which negative to print. Well, I've obviously picked the one in which I cut down most of the undergrowth.

I took this with a fairly long lens to stay back from the building and also to include just this little bit of tree because the sky was totally bald. Having something like that to carry you back into the picture helps a lot. This was done with a 4 × 5 from a tripod, very carefully composed. I was probably at least an hour on this site doing this picture because I waited for the sunlight to come down and hit the front door.

132. Camp meeting, Smith Island, Maryland, July 28, 1991 MSA SC 1890-BP-25,174

Camp meeting on Smith Island is an annual event. It starts on one Sunday, and they have a prayer service every night during the week, and then it closes with another service the following Sunday. A revival service is really what it is, and they have a guest preacher. There was a black man from Wesley Theological Seminary preaching this year, and they'd imported an organ from Delaware that came over in the boat with me.

People come from all over the country back to Smith Island. At every third or fourth house, somebody's having a family reunion, and the food is really good, too. Louis Goldstein and the senators, the whole bunch of them, showed up on that first Sunday. They all came down on a boat and got off and walked up there and stayed for the service, and then they went somewhere to eat.

It's an old custom. I remember in Missouri the Methodists would have their revival

meeting once a year and people would come home to it, but I don't think it's done in the modern church very much.

I was told I wasn't going to be allowed to photograph the actual camp meeting, but the services had not started. They were singing hymns, waiting for somebody to come in, so they didn't mind my taking a photograph.

133. Carnival at North Beach, Maryland, August 24, 1985 MSA SC 1890-BP-20,197

I was attracted by the spontaneity of these women as they interacted with each other, their expressive faces, and their obvious preoccupation with motherhood. It's amazing how fast clothing can date a picture. Right now these styles look perfectly normal; in ten years, this picture will look very dated. In thirty years, it will be a documentary record of how women of various generations dressed in the eighties.

These women were completely unaware of me or my camera even though it was set up on a tripod. I got only one exposure before they shifted positions and some of them moved on. I like this kind of photography, where the camera captures a moment of real life.

133. Hanging out on Smith Island, Maryland, July 26, 1991 MSA SC 1890-BP-25,068

It was late in the afternoon, just before evening, and the children of the town were gathered at Ruke's store. You could call it the crossroads of Ewell, Maryland. Other than running up and down the road in their cars, this is probably the social life of the town for kids.

The kids drive back and forth between Ewell and Rhodes Point in their automobiles, playing chicken to a certain extent and also just for the hell of it. They often stop on the road and speak to people. It's something to be going down the road in the car and have the car ahead of you just suddenly stop. And a car coming the other way stops too and blocks traffic for five minutes while they talk. That's not unusual at all, and nobody does anything about it. Nobody cares because it's part of the way of life there.

Hardly anybody goes anywhere who doesn't get in the car, even to go down the street to the neighbor's. In the town of Ewell, you can walk from one end of it to the other in five minutes, but most people get in the car and drive. Few of the cars have mufflers, so you don't have to worry about getting hit walking; you can easily hear the "Vvvrrrmmmmm" of a car coming without a muffler.

134. St. Elizabeth's Roman Catholic Church, Westover, Maryland, May 11, 1986 MSA SC 1890-BP-6974-2

For several years I was preoccupied with commercial and industrial assignments, so I didn't have the time to do documentary photographs the way I once had. It wasn't until I began the Bay Project that I really started saturation shooting again, recording every aspect of life on and near the Chesapeake.

St. Elizabeth's Church is near my daughter's home in Somerset County, and we go to church there sometimes. This Sunday I set up the 4 × 5 camera across the street before Mass, then went inside for the service. When it was over, I ran out and got to the camera as the people were coming out.

135. First Baptist Church, near Mathews, Virginia, March 30, 1993 MSA SC 1890-BP-26,508

The first time I saw this steeple it was raining. A pattern like this does not photograph very well in soft light. The next afternoon when I came back by there, the sun had come out, so I stopped and made pictures.

I was there at just the right time, when the crosslighting on the steeple was bringing out the texture of the shingles. In flat lighting, all this sort of runs together, but with the sunlight, you get the shadows that make the patterns stand out.

135. St. James African Methodist Episcopal Church, Oriole, Maryland, April 1, 1991 MSA SC 1890-BP-24,884

Oriole is only a broad stretch in the road, with maybe a dozen or so houses and a little country store or two, a filling station. This is a deserted black church with a leaking roof, the siding off, and the floor pretty well gone out of it. The black community is trying to raise money to restore it because it's a very fine example of a black community church on the Eastern Shore. It's going to be a major restoration job.

I purposely included the tops of the three windows on the first floor so that it readily identifies as a church. When I did this picture, I also did any number of pictures of the

I miss oysters. My son once in a while will bring me a few. A while ago he came by with one of those little plastic dishes about half full. He said, "That's what I caught in my dredge." He said, "Maybe you can get you two cakes of oysters." So I did. I stretched them with Jiffy Mix. I don't know what's going to happen unless the Lord intervenes. He's the one that put them there in the first place, and He can clean them up and put more there. That's the only hope. VIRGINIA EVANS

church cemetery and the church itself, but this dramatic detail probably speaks to the whole church better than just having a record shot of the entire building.

136. Knapps Narrows, Tilghman Island, Maryland, March 5, 1987
MSA SC 1890-BP-7263

I was down at Tilghman Island in March with the Chesapeake Bay Foundation to give a lecture to their field instructors at Harrison's Restaurant. It was one of those bitter, bitter cold March days. On that kind of a day you often get a heavy cloud cover with the light breaking through and streaking. I decided that this was so typical of a winter day on the Eastern Shore that I took the picture.

I guess I've been colder, but I can't remember when. This was taken from the roof of my van, which made me exposed to the wind that much more. I waited for the streaks of light through the clouds and carefully planned each of these boats to recede so that the viewer would look across at the sky. When I got down, my fingers were hurting so that I went down to the nearest little restaurant and had a hot chocolate and tried to thaw them out. It was probably half an hour before they didn't just absolutely hurt with cold. But I think the picture was worth it.

The three boats in the foreground lie almost totally separate from one another, giving you a pattern. And each of them has long hand tongs. Across the narrows you see some housing and boatyards, as well as three skipjacks in a row. But the strongest thing about this scene is the winter sky. You don't see a sky like this in the summertime. See the seagull up there on the pole? I always like to get a little bit of life in so it isn't completely sterile.

136–137. Skiffs, Shady Side, Maryland, August 12, 1985
MSA SC 1890-BP-20,112

This photograph is a good example of my belief that when you see a picture, you should always stop and take it right then because it probably won't be there when you return. Dramatic lighting like this is usually a one-time opportunity. I've been back to this scene numerous times, but it's never looked so rustic again; the pier has been modernized and has lost some of its visual appeal. I will probably never point my camera this way again.

138–139. Wetlands anchorage near Deal Island, Maryland, c. 1951
MSA SC 1890-MI-1290

I've always liked this picture of a crab skiff pulled up in a drainage ditch. I don't know why this boat was there or what the access to the main river was. I also don't know what these two poles are down there for. Maybe they're to load something aboard the boat. I wasn't smart enough in those days to figure it out myself or to ask the right question.

I think boats now are mainly down at docks, at marinas, but this used to be, I don't say commonplace, but it wasn't unusual. I stopped on this scene because I liked the vast area and the loblollies off in the distance and the reflection of the boat.

140. Upside down, Tylerton, Maryland, September 29, 1991
MSA SC 1890-BP-7003

This picture has a story. My daughter Mame had been after me to do more 4 × 5s rather than the small format size because they're sharper and because she likes big negatives. So with due respect to her and her desires, I decided that I would take the 4 × 5 to Smith Island.

The second day there, I had my equipment all open so I could just set it up on the tripod, when I saw this deadrise, *Miss Yvonne*, tied up at the dock near another boat up on land and an overturned rowboat, and I said, "Now that's a nice composition." I got the camera out, and the minute I started to set it up, *Miss Yvonne* left the dock. I could see that he was going to go out and back up and then come by me again, so I quickly focused the camera and got ready. I exposed the film just when the boat was clearing the house, but before the bow had gone out of the picture. I may have gotten a better picture than I would have had the boat been tied up along here.

But my point is that had I been working with my smaller camera, I would not only have gotten the picture I wanted, because I'd have been ready the minute I picked the camera up, but I would have gotten this picture, too. So the 4 × 5 does slow you down, and frankly speaking, I question whether you're going to be able to tell which was made with a 4 × 5 and which was made with a 120 camera.

140. Bavon, Virginia, March 30, 1993 MSA SC 1890-BP-26,526

We were waiting for the last boat of the season that was dredging crabs to come in. Over across Davis Creek was this lovely view of a marina with a lot of workboats. Every boat but one in this picture is a wooden boat.

The rounded cabin and rounded stern are distinctive of a Virginia boat. The way the water flows makes them more efficient there. Even the length of the boat has an impact on how it performs, so Virginians have developed a boat that works well in their waters.

141. Clam rigs, Broad Creek, Deltaville, Virginia, March 29, 1993
MSA SC 1890-BP-26,443

This was a foggy, drizzly day, which was probably why the boats were in. A father and son operate these two boats. One boat has rigs on both sides; the other has a rig only on one side.

142–143. Inner Harbor, Baltimore, Maryland, August 22, 1984
MSA SC 1890-MI-7070

One afternoon I got a call from the Baltimore convention bureau saying that the *Pride of Baltimore* would be sailing out of the harbor the next morning. This was a rare occurrence for several reasons. The *Pride* wasn't in Baltimore very often; she was usually sailing around the world as a good will ambassador for the city. When she was there, she usually left under power because it's not easy to maneuver around the other boats when you're relying on the wind. Now, of course, this picture is all the more special because the original *Pride* was lost at sea some time later.

At this particular time, the Rusty Scupper restaurant overlooking the Inner Harbor had just opened. I had discovered while it was under construction that I could get a very commanding view of the skyline from its roof, so I called the owners and got permission to be up there when the *Pride* sailed by. I like this vantage point because the marina on the left helps to anchor the picture and implies that Baltimore is a center for pleasure boating as well as a big city.

143. Baltimore & Ohio Railroad piers at Locust Point, Baltimore, Maryland, c. 1960 MSA SC 1890-MI-14,374

Back when I was the official photographer for the Maryland Port Authority, occasionally we would use a helicopter to document the port as it was at that particular time, knowing full well that the whole scene would change as the port was improved and developed. We're looking across the ships to the B&O grain elevators, the train tracks, the freight cars; and over the Domino Sugar towers you see downtown Baltimore. At that time the only tall building in downtown Baltimore was the Matheson Building, which became the Maryland National Bank building. Charles Center had not been built yet.

We're near Fort McHenry, flying in a helicopter just above the ships, which gives you a very nice perspective on the depth of the yard and the distance to the city.

144–145. Aircraft carriers *John F. Kennedy* and *America* berthed at Norfolk, Virginia, July 30, 1993 MSA SC 1890-BP-26,984

My friend Tom Horton has always emphasized the importance of the federal presence on the Chesapeake Bay, so I went to the Newport News–Norfolk area to record a symbol of this important influence. This picture could only have been taken at Norfolk because nowhere else on the Bay would you see giant aircraft carriers side by side. The ships were backlighted, creating strong silhouettes and giving an almost ominous impression. I had envisioned a frontlighted, detailed picture of the carriers, but we got there at high noon and since the ships are battleship grey, that was impossible. I think it worked out for the best, though, because this photograph conveys the message I had in mind.

145. Sunrise on the Wye River at Bennett Point, Maryland, c. 1988
MSA SC 1890-BP-7048A

Bennett Point is one of my very favorite places to go to make photographs because there are a lot of workboats tied up there. There's a public dock where watermen can bring in their pickup trucks and take their product off the boat and haul it to market. I also like it that you're looking across at Wye Island where there are no houses. You don't have telephone poles or distractions in the background; you have a very pristine area to photograph.

This was taken at early morning, probably before seven o'clock. I have a rule of thumb: The only time you can photograph directly into the sun is when the sun

The Chesapeake Bay is holding its own. There's no way it can ever be like it used to be because there's too many people. But it does look better, the water and all. I think they're doing some things that's helping, but it takes so much money to do anything anymore that whether they'll be able to stay with it, I don't know. Hopefully, it will last a while. It's a shame to have all that pretty water out there and only be able to ride around in it on a boat. BOBBY MC KAY

doesn't disturb you to look at it. It was hazy enough this particular morning that I knew I could make a picture right into the sun.

I got the path of the sun coming at the shore right between a boat that's been turned over and a couple of rowboats and then I framed it with an old pine tree in the foreground.

Causes and Cures

146. Hackett Point, Anne Arundel County, Maryland, May 17, 1986

MSA SC 1890-BP-20,834

When I was in China, I was impressed by how many people were working the fields. Here you have a tractor that's harrowing the field. This one man can do that whole field in probably a couple of hours, where in China, it's ten people hand-doing it. With mechanized farming today, it's amazing how little time the farmer actually stays out in the field on any given day.

Even when you do see them, they often have these huge tractors that are air-conditioned, and some of them, I understand, even have televisions in them. They go up and down these fields, and the man is hidden completely in a cabin, sitting up high. There's not very much human relationship to the land.

This John Deere tractor was stirring up such a cloud of dust that you could see absolutely nothing behind it. This piece of land is right at the edge of the Chesapeake Bay below the Bay bridge, so all this dirt going into the air was blowing directly out into the Bay.

You might say that a little bit of dirt doesn't matter, but year after year it adds up to a great deal of topsoil going out to sea and being lost.

148. Back Creek, Annapolis, Maryland, August 22, 1985

MSA SC 1890-BP-7053

These crab boats are tied up at a wharf over on the south side of Back Creek, and across the creek, you see all the masts—you couldn't begin to count them, really—of modern sailboats. When we came to Annapolis, there were no modern sailboats on Back Creek at all, no marinas, and any docks that were there were just like this little dock in the foreground. To me, this is very symbolic of the fact that the sailboat and power boats are taking over the creek, and the one remaining little vestige of native boats is being overwhelmed by the progress of pleasure boats.

148. Oil in grasses, Powhatan Creek, Jamestown, Virginia, July 31,

1993 MSA SC 1890-BP-27,035

We were crossing the bridge to Jamestown Island, when Mame spotted this oil on the water. Here we are looking straight down off the bridge into the water, and you can see a great deal of floating oil. There were boat facilities a quarter mile upcreek.

This photograph gives a very dramatic picture of the amount of oil that comes down from a marina and eventually winds up in the James and then, of course, in the Chesapeake Bay.

Color probably would have helped to show the oil more distinctly, because oil reflects color and there was quite a bit of sky reflected off the oil.

148–149. Fishing on the Susquehanna Flats, August 11, 1963

MSA SC 1890-MI-1583

I was flying above the Susquehanna Flats near Havre de Grace, working on an exhibit for the Department of Natural Resources about fishing on the Chesapeake Bay, when I saw this collection of boats. These boats all cluster together where the fish are running; they all want to be where the fish are. I also think some people want to be in groups rather than isolated.

In the foreground is a little houseboat with a wake behind it. It was a traveling hot dog stand. They would go from boat to boat selling hot dogs and hamburgers and soda pop. There were enough boats out there for them to make a living at it.

150. Warren's Ferry, Virginia, July 14, 1993 MSA SC 1890-BP-7021

This was made in the upper reaches of the James River, where the river is comparatively narrow. It's fresh water there, so you have fresh water grasses rather than salt water grasses. The grasses almost form islands with the hills in the background, so you

know this is not in the tidewater area. You also see some rapids here, which show that the river is quite shallow at this point.

In order to be able to see the water in the foreground, it was necessary to cut some weeds down. My faithful helper, Mame, took the machete that I always carry along and chopped, while I stood at the camera and directed her: "Get that one there." "No, that one's still a little too high." "There's a straggly one down there." When I was satisfied that they were cut down enough, I said, "Okay, now we take the picture." But I purposely left some of them, particularly on the left side of the picture, not only to show the height, but because they added depth to the photograph.

150–151. James River at Richmond, Virginia, July 15, 1993

MSA SC 1890-BP-7015

Normally when you find a city skyline, you've got all kinds of debris in the foreground or you have to get permission to get up in a building to get a good vantage point. Here in Richmond, I found this wonderful ramp that was built just for that purpose—to have a view of the skyline. It's part of the new flood control system they're building because of the flash floods that come down the James River and inundate the lower end of town.

Richmond has become quite a metropolis. During the last few years many of these buildings have been completed and it's now beginning to look like a major city. I like the fact that I included one of the old bridges across the river. It gives that appearance of the old city. That little bit of land in the foreground shows the width of the river.

Richmond is quite a ways up the James from the Chesapeake. It's a little more obvious at Richmond that the city will have an effect on the Bay than it is in Charlottesville, but Charlottesville, too, is in the watershed of the Chesapeake. They're both far enough upriver that you might think they don't have the effect that, say, Baltimore does, but they do. It's all downstream to the Bay.

152. Anne Arundel County, Maryland, August 6, 1992 MSA SC 1890-BP-6922A

As I go down the road, I often see things that are potential photographs. One of the things that I see is the encroachment of housing on farm land like this scene with two tobacco barns in the backyard of a very modern house with a two-car garage and a pickup truck and two automobiles sitting out front.

The first time I made this picture, I didn't get what I wanted. A man came out and wanted to know what I was taking the picture for, and I explained, and he said it was his son-in-law who built this house and he wasn't very happy about it, but he had given his daughter the land, I guess, or sold it to her, and this type of house was built.

The second time, we got there around five o'clock on a summer afternoon, and the light was not yet right on the building. By the time I got the tripod out and got everything ready, the light began to creep onto the front of the building very nicely, and it gave me the dramatic effect I wanted.

It's a fact of life that farm land is being gobbled up by development. This looks more like a house that people who work in the city would live in. I mean, farmers just don't build this style house. That old farmer said, "God, I wouldn't have built a house like that. Look at that great big window up there over the door. That'll let more cold in. You got to think about those things." That's what a farmer would think. The city dweller doesn't care so much about what the utility bill is, he wants more aesthetics than practicality in a house.

152–153. The Downs on the Severn River, 1991

MSA SC 1890-BP-7027

The property where The Downs is now was for many years the golf course at Sherwood Forest, which is an old summer-home development on the Severn River.

A few years ago, the golf course was taken over for development, and as a result, we have these huge houses along the river. They've stripped the shoreline of all foliage and put bulkheading in, and a lot of natural sea grasses have been lost. When you spend a million dollars on a piece of property, you don't want any of it to erode away, and you want to have a lawn all the way down with a clear view of the river. It's interesting that these houses are so close together; everybody wants his piece of the view.

153. Power, Anne Arundel County, Maryland, October 16, 1985

MSA SC 1890-BP-20,376

This power line goes into the naval station on the Severn River. They were increasing the voltage significantly, so they had three big cherry pickers there with men in all of the baskets. Fortunately, it was a very clear day, so I made this in both color transparency and in black and white. I picked an angle where you can see the men working where you also get a good cross-section of the rigging and the poles.

The low angle shows only a base of trees, not houses or other poles off in the distance, and the crosslighting gives a very dramatic effect. It was all very carefully planned to get a diagonal sweep through the photograph, which adds action to it. Horizontal lines always signify complacency and quiet; diagonals imply action.

I thought this picture was symbolic of the increased population, the increased development of the area. After all, the average country neighborhood doesn't have all these power lines, so obviously the power is being supplied for industry or for a lot of housing.

154. Turbines at Conowingo Dam, Conowingo, Maryland, September 3, 1986 MSA SC 1890-BP-21,226

The Susquehanna River is dammed at Conowingo, and the water goes through the turbines and generates electricity. It's the only hydroelectric plant in Maryland, but it's actually owned by the Pennsylvania Power and Light Company, and it serves a lot of the area up into Pennsylvania.

The power company just put in a fish ladder to let the fish go up the river to spawn. If they went through the turbines they'd be cut up, and so there are screens to keep them out.

There's a balcony overlooking the turbines where you stand as they conduct tours. I just rested the camera on the ledge of the balcony and made this photograph; that's daylight coming in through the windows.

154–155. Three Mile Island nuclear power plant, Pennsylvania, May 30, 1988 MSA SC 1890-BP-22,418

Three Mile Island has become the symbol of nuclear accidents. I was driving up along the Susquehanna, and I saw this off in the distance. I decided I would get as close to Three Mile Island as I could, and I found this park right across the river from the island.

I wanted something in the picture that gave the human element in contrast to the nuclear plant, and here came these two fishermen in a little aluminum powerboat chugging up the river, so I snapped the shutter, showing them in the foreground with this monster of Three Mile Island behind them.

I talked to some people who live there about being right under the cooling towers of the nuclear plant, and they think nothing of it. I said, "How about property values?" And one person said, "Oh, after the accident, things did drop off for a while, but they're back to normal now."

I was actually going up by Harrisburg when I heard about the Three Mile Island accident, and I thought to myself, "If there's any loss into the Susquehanna River, the whole Chesapeake Bay will be wiped out." I think it should never have been built there for that reason.

156. Waterskiing on Back River near Jamestown, Virginia, July 30, 1993 MSA SC 1890-BP-27,021

We were in the narrow passage that separates Jamestown Island from the mainland, observing the fallen trees and erosion on both shores, when this motorboat sped by. Its considerable wake washed against the shore and was a violation of the five-mile-an-hour, No Wake sign that was just behind me as I took the picture.

156. Erosion on the Choptank River, September 1, 1986
MSA SC 1890-BP-20,691

Apparently this tree had been dead long before it fell down, and it's lying out about twenty feet from the bank, and then there's another one off in the distance that's even farther out from the bank. The significance here is obviously that the bank is eroded back. You wouldn't have to go to this site to realize that at one time those trees probably stood up right where they are. I have no idea how long it took the bank to get back where it is here, but you see the grass hanging over the edge and the ravines coming down that mean that the dirt and soil is washing away. The bank is about ten or twelve feet back from the beach, so you know that in storms the waters come up a good deal higher than this picture shows. Since this photograph was taken, they have put in riprap to stop the erosion.

Erosion does two things. One, it eats away the farmer's land. He's losing land every time there's a storm. But more important is this soil is going out into the Chesapeake and silting up the Bay.

157. Blackwalnut Point, Tilghman Island, Maryland, November 11, 1989 MSA SC 1890-BP-23,042

My wife and some friends and I went down and stayed at a bed and breakfast at Blackwalnut Point. It's right on the end of Tilghman Island and you can look out at the Bay and the mouth of the Choptank River.

I thought this was a pretty good example of riprap on the edge of an island because I had big stones in the foreground, good lighting, and a view out to sea. It makes a good statement about protecting your shoreline.

158–159. Erosion at Elliott's Island, Maryland, October 2, 1993
MSA SC 1890-BP-27,083

Fishing Bay is an estuary off the lower Chesapeake where the seas can get pretty rough. This day the wind was blowing the surf right against the shore and you can see how it's eroding the dirt away. That little bit of grass is trying hard to hold the soil in place. There's some bulkheading at the far end of the picture, but a lot has already eroded away.

This was early October, and you can imagine how much more severe it would be when a storm came through in the wintertime. There was a house about a hundred yards behind me and an old overstuffed chair down by the water, so I imagine the resident comes down and watches the sun go down.

This was taken at about ten o'clock in the morning with the light coming in from the east. Backlighting gives a lot more detail to the foam and the splash of the water, and the sunlight plays off the waves.

160. Lumber mill near Goochland, Virginia, July 15, 1993
MSA SC 1890-BP-26,816

These ten-foot lengths of wood were stacked in different piles as far as the eye could see. I took the picture from the top of my van so I could see over some of the stacks to other stacks off in the distance. Had I done it from ground level, we'd only see the things that were right around me.

I included the piece of equipment to give scale. When you see a piece of equipment like that with tracks around it, it's obvious that man is involved in it. Even though I don't actually have the man visible in the picture, it's pretty obvious that he has his hand in what's going on and this isn't wood that's just stacked till eternity off in some storage area.

This scene is less than half a mile from the James River. These are pine saplings and pine runoff is quite acid. The scrap and sawdust left here undoubtedly adds a lot more acidity to the river.

160–161. Debris from clear-cutting timber on the road to Crisfield from Pocomoke, Maryland, May 28, 1989 MSA SC 1890-BP-22,744

Here is an area that was stripped for lumber. You see what's left after the logs were hauled off to the mill: the branches and limbs of the trees that were cut and a few undesirable trees. Eventually, a bulldozer will push all this into one huge pile, and then they'll burn it. This may lie here for years like this before they burn it, until they have some other use for the land.

Every one of the trees that stood here, and the leaves that fell from them, stopped the flow of water. When it rained hard, most of the water soaked into the ground. Now a lot is going to run off. After they bulldoze, even more will run off. When the new field is planted with crops, the insecticides and all the other things that are put into the land will wash down to the stream, too.

162–163. Hopewell, Virginia, July 15, 1993 MSA SC 1890-BP-26,794

Right now I think Allied Signal is a pretty clean operation, but at one time it created a lot of pollution. I went to Hopewell because I knew that Kepone had been discharged there and that the James River had been closed because of that. The name Hopewell became synonymous with pollution.

164. Charlie's chickens, Somerset County, Maryland, October 1990
MSA SC 1890-BP-24,314

There's an awful lot of maintenance to a chicken house because they have feeders and pipes that pass food and water all the way down the full length of it. In the bottom of each window is a fan. In the summertime, the fans ventilate the house.

This was an extremely difficult picture to make because the light level is low in the chicken house and the chickens are very flighty, so that if you raise your arm to scratch

*Crabs look good for another year. And the oyster business, I still say it's going to come back in. I
wish the governors of Maryland and Virginia both could get together on it. Let them tong up to
Christmas and keep them on the limit like you've got it. And after Christmas, allow everybody with
a little dredge to drag this bottom over. Put them on a strict limit, a limit that they can make a living
at it, and then drag the bottom. It'll do more good than anything in this Bay that I know of.*

EDWARD HARRISON

your head, the chickens are going to flutter and move. Then you have to wait for them to settle down again, and it means sometimes standing there three or four minutes.

I put a couple of extra lights down the length of the chicken house to show how big it is and to show that the chickens go as far as the eye can see. The lighting problem is complicated by the fact that these moving chickens stir up a dust and there's a continual haze, which means that your depth becomes a little softer.

These chickens are moving all the time, they're overlapping one another, they're bobbing their heads. So you've got to take a lot of trial-and-error photographs in order to get one with the chickens in the foreground wire sharp without a lot of movement.

164–165. Dairy farm near Olney, Maryland, October 1986

MSA SC 1890-BP-21,449

I particularly like this scene because it shows a comparatively modern cow barn and a nice herd of cattle all tied in one composition. Photographing animals is tough, particularly in groups, because they overlap one another, and they get all confused, and they turn their rear ends to you. Here all the cows are in pretty good shape, though some are lying down. It's a typical herd of cattle in a rolling countryside. It's away from the water up in Montgomery County, but the runoff from these cows' manure actually goes into streams and eventually winds up in the Chesapeake Bay.

166–167. No-till farming near Easton, Maryland, April 12, 1986

MSA SC 1890-BP-20,730

This shows no-till farming. It was taken off Route 50, just short of Easton. No-till farming is exactly what the name implies. You don't plow the ground. By not plowing the ground, there's obviously less runoff of topsoil when the seeds are planted and the moisture is held there by the undergrowth that's on the ground.

The containers on the plow, behind the tractor, contain liquid fertilizer, and there's a digger that digs a hole in the ground and drops in some fertilizer and seed.

You see that the weeds from the previous year are still there, and the seeds are being planted right on top of them. This can only be done about three years in a row. After that the ground gets so hard the seeds won't come up.

167. Farmers checking the gauge at a water station, Warsaw, Virginia, August 7, 1991 MSA SC 1890-BP-21,162

The Chesapeake Bay Foundation had a meeting of farmers at Warsaw, Virginia, down near the Rappahannock, to study soil conditions and erosion. We got on buses and went from one farm to another, one location to another.

This is a water station on a small stream. The box that you see up in the upper part of the picture has instruments in it that go down into the water and measure the water depth every hour. When it rains, the instruments take samples of how much sediment washes into the water and what the sediment is.

I'm standing on a bridge that crosses the little stream. The stream is about four feet wide now, but sometimes it comes up over the sandbagging and stones.

One of the most interesting things we saw on this particular trip was an acre of land planted in soybeans. One side was no-till, the other was plowed. There were pipes mounted over the whole acre and they turned the water on, like rainfall, equally on both halves, and showered it down for about five, ten minutes.

They measured the amount of runoff and sediment and it was very impressive to see how much more sediment there was in the water that came from where the land had been plowed. It looked chocolatey. On the no-till side, there was very little sediment runoff because the rain had soaked in. This was a very graphic demonstration of the advantages of no-till.

168. Anacostia neighborhood clean-up project, Bladensburg, Maryland, October 22, 1990 MSA SC 1890-BP-24,334

This photograph was taken over on the Anacostia River. It was a Saturday in the autumn, a special day of tree planting and cleaning up the Anacostia. The governor was there, and a number of other people from Chesapeake Bay Affairs, and a lot of kids came. The bulldozer helped to clear land, and everybody was digging holes and planting trees. Even somebody in a wheelchair helped to plant a tree.

169. Chesapeake Bay Foundation educational cruise, Rhode River, May 31, 1986 MSA SC 1890-BP-20,887

The Chesapeake Bay Foundation takes schoolchildren out to take samplings from the bottom of the Bay and analyze them and learn firsthand about what Bay life is like.

This was a school group from up in Pennsylvania. They were busy studying plankton and various other life brought up out of the Bay.

The students were quite interested in what was going on. Here I show a little bit of the shoreline as well as other boats. You get a pretty good idea that this is a hands-on learning experience on the Bay.

Some of these children probably had never been out on the water before, let alone on a skipjack, so it was quite a thrilling experience for them. I was impressed with how seriously they took it. The students were told what they were apt to find in the Bay—oysters crabs, and various other life—and that each was interdependent with the others. They would throw over a trawl and bring it up with whatever was in it. Then they would lay it out on the deck, and the instructors would explain what each form of life was. They would say, "Is that all you see?" "Is that all there is?" Most of the kids would say yes and the instructors would tell them, "No, that's only the beginning." And they would get down to the microscopic life and explain how it was food for the bigger fish and crustaceans. It was quite an educational program.

169. Tom Wisner and Mary Sue Kaelin, January 1987 MSA SC 1890-BP-22,459

Tom Wisner spent a good many years with the biological lab down in Solomons. Now he goes around to festivals and sings his songs of the Chesapeake. "Chesapeake Born" is his most famous song. In fact, when the *National Geographic* did a special on the region, they introduced it with "Chesapeake Born."

Tom's friend, Mary Sue, has a nice voice that goes well with his. They go to schools to put on performances about the Bay and entertain the kids. I've seen him do these a number of times, and he really relates to the kids. The kids just love him, and I think they get a great deal out of it. He'll explain the difference between a male crab and a female crab, for instance, and how you can tell.

170. Planting oyster shells, James River, July 30, 1993 MSA SC 1890-BP-26,897

We were quite lucky to run into this situation on the lower James. The Virginia Marine Resources Commission was planting fresh oyster shells on an oyster bed. This is a barge with oyster shells heaped upon it that had been towed into position, and then with a powerful hose, these oyster shells were being washed overboard, much as you'd wash leaves off your sidewalk. The barge was going back and forth, and they were planting them in a very definite area.

Now, that doesn't mean larvae will all strike and take hold, but they keep trying. What it does mean is that the water is clean enough to support an oyster bed, and that's a good sign in itself, because the water's been tested. Whether the oysters take or not is another story. Now, this is the James River, which was closed for many years because of Kepone that was discharged. For years this river was totally closed to this type of operation—fishing, clamming, oystering—and to swimming. So this is a very hopeful sign that the river is considered safe enough to do this.

171. Governors Harry Hughes and Charles Robb inspecting an oyster bed near Irvington, Virginia, September 20, 1985 MSA SC 1890-BP-20,359

I was on a helicopter tour of Pennsylvania, Maryland, and Virginia with the three governors, who were making a tour of the condition of the Bay. We landed at the country club at Irvington, where we took off in boats and went up this river. Now the way the organizers explained it, this was an oyster bed that had been contaminated and was just being re-opened that year for oystering. They opened an oyster and offered it to Governor Hughes, and he said, no, he wouldn't eat an oyster, he didn't trust it. So Governor Robb ate it. He had little choice in the matter since it was a Virginia oyster.

This was very much a staged event and it made good coverage for the newspapers, but those governors didn't really see much of the condition of the Bay, believe me. However, I thought it was important to show that our politicians were concerned about the Bay.

171. Wetlands development protest, Back Bay, near Shady Side, Maryland, September 14, 1992 MSA SC 1890-BP-26,062

These people have come out to protest a development on the West River. They're particularly against building houses on wetlands. Contractors bring in tons and tons of fill dirt so they can pour a basement in it. When it gets wet, everybody's house is on an island, except for the driveway that goes out to the road. You might say, "How come they're permitted to do this?" Well, these permits were gotten before the laws against building in wetlands went into effect. Of course you know there're always more sides to these things than meet the eye. Many homes along the Bay were built before we all were so conscious about destroying wetlands, and sometimes their owners are the ones protesting more development of the wetlands.

You can't let your heart sink or the fire die in your belly. You've got to keep going and hope that you'll make a difference ultimately in what the end result is. It's just a shame and a disgrace and I guess it's a sin on the heads of all of us that we've allowed things to deteriorate the way they have. We did it because we were ignorant and we didn't know any better. That is no longer an excuse. We know now what we're doing wrong. We know what has to be done. What we have to do is make that the top priority and get on and get the job done. BERNIE FOWLER

When I went down to make pictures, the contractor who was building this development came along in a pickup truck, and he stopped to talk to me. I took the neutral position and said, "I'm just documenting what you're doing here as a matter of record." He said, speaking of the person who was leading the protest, "I built her house twenty years ago, and we had to fill in wetlands to build it." Now she's one of the big champions of the wetlands. And yet she lives in the wetlands. So I don't know. It's almost a case of if you've got yours, you don't want anybody else to infringe upon it.

172–173. Middle River, September 1985 MSA SC 1890-BP-6945

I like this picture because it shows the manmade ditches that drain a little bit of the wetlands on Middle River above Baltimore. The trees look like they're twenty to fifty years old, but the rest is all marshy wetlands until you get to the upper end of the picture. There you see a development of houses right on the shoreline and a railroad bridge across Middle River to Baltimore.

When you're on ground level, it's hard to visualize the tributaries, the estuaries, and all the wetlands. This really shows you what a delicate balance there is between open water and marshy land and then solid ground. I'm sure that in the wintertime, especially, this area is teeming with wildlife.

173. Osprey, Assateague, Virginia, July 1969 MSA SC 1890-MI-10,206

Dave Hamilton, a photographer friend, and I had gone down to Assateague to take down an exhibit at the visitors center. Mr. Apple, the superintendent, mentioned that they had nursed an injured osprey back to health and were about to release it. He offered to let us photograph it first.

A shot like this could only be made on 35 mm because the bird was bobbing up and down the whole time. I shot it on Kodachrome and converted it to 4 × 5 black and white. My philosophy then, when I had to choose between color or black and white, was to shoot color because I could always convert later.

Pleasant Living

174. Harbor at St. Michaels, Maryland, September 26, 1986

MSA SC 1890-BP-22,532

We had anchored in St. Michaels harbor overnight, and I was up at dawn watching the fog lift when this oyster boat passed us, maneuvering quietly among the visiting yachts anchored in the harbor. Many of my more dramatic photographs have been made as daylight breaks. The water is usually calm and gives strong reflections. Here the wake created by the workboat adds action to a tranquil scene.

176–177. Yacht race, Chesapeake Bay, c. 1953 MSA SC 1890-MI-1621

I'm always amused by this picture because its success was so unintentional. The Naval Academy had commissioned me to make a photograph of its sailing squadron. It was the last weekend of the fall racing series, and although the wind was good, it was a terribly overcast day.

Just for the heck of it, I loaded some infrared film. When I was out on the water I was pretty desperate, trying to figure out how to get some drama out of such a dull sky. Having completely forgotten about the infrared film, I used a red filter and compensated with a long exposure.

I went home convinced I had nothing, but when I developed the film and looked at it, I was amazed to see this cloud bank because I certainly hadn't seen it in the sky. Only then did I realize my mistake. The academy was thrilled and ordered a huge mural.

178. Yachts near Annapolis, Maryland, c. 1958 MSA SC 1890-MI-923

Barlovento and *Freedom* were participating in a race from the mouth of the Severn River to Cove Point. All of the boats—there were about ten of them—were very large, and these races were held in the fall or winter because that's the time when there's enough wind for them.

I went out on a powerboat to about five miles beyond the starting point and waited for them. In a race like this, the yachts usually don't get close enough for you to get more than one of them in a picture this close up, but I had my skipper maneuver to bring these two together and into the path of the sun. We were moving at about twelve knots and the yachts were going faster.

It was cold as blazes out there, and keeping the spray off of my camera—a handheld 4 × 5—wasn't easy. That's something you need to learn to do on a boat: know when

spray is coming. You have to be able to anticipate it or your equipment will get soaked. Sometimes I keep the camera under my windbreaker; sometimes I just turn quickly and let the spray hit me on the back.

178–179. Racing aboard *Freedom*, Chesapeake Bay, c. 1955

MSA SC 1890-MI-1609

This was taken in my more agile days. I was aboard the Naval Academy's old wooden schooner, *Freedom*, and I crawled out on the bowsprit, which put me about fifteen feet out in front of the actual boat. I was looking back at the entire boat, and the wake it was making meant we were going at a good clip. This was taken during a race, on what's called a long reach, and the crew was just sitting around drinking coffee, which makes the picture quite informal.

180. Spa Creek, October 1987 MSA SC 1890-BP-30,286

I saw this scene just after we moved into town when I was riding my bike one day on Lafayette Avenue. I got up before dawn the next morning and went back and shot a whole series of pictures as the sun was coming up, until it got too bright for the lens. After all these years of taking water views in Annapolis, it's still exciting when I discover a new vista.

180–181. Fog on Spa Creek, October 15, 1992 MSA SC 1890-BP-26,142

My daughter Mame called me up one morning and said, "Hey, there's a great fog out there. Go do some pictures." She knew I was probably hunkered down in the darkroom. Well, you don't just go out and do fog pictures. You've got to have a little cooperation from things. I drove down to the foot of Southgate Avenue, and here was the sun just breaking through the fog behind these boats that were anchored. Out of the corner of my eye, I saw some people getting into a dinghy. One of the things I didn't like about the situation was that the reflection was perfect. I wanted something to disturb the water a little bit. As the dinghy moved through my path of sunlight, I snapped this one picture.

You've got to be ready when you want to make a picture like this because if you hesitate one second, it's too late. This photograph had to have perfect conditions. Without the sun's image there and the reflection of the water, it would have been very flat. On the other hand, if the fog had lifted a little more, the sun would have been so bright that I couldn't shoot directly into it. You can't always count on getting a picture like this just by going out in the fog.

182–183. Log canoe racing, Tred Avon River, c. 1964

MSA SC 1890-MI-839 (35 mm)

This is a closeup that shows all the activity of log canoeing. It shows the helmsman, the man who's bailing water out of the boat, and all of the people who have crawled out on the hiking boards to balance the boat and keep it from capsizing. There is nothing in the background except landscape, which makes it a very simple photograph.

This was done with a 200 mm lens on 35 mm film, a pretty long telephoto. It's just about as long as you can handhold, particularly on a boat. This would be almost impossible to do with a larger format camera.

You can't get that close to these log canoes because they need a lot of room to maneuver and you never know when they're going to come about. You can make yourself very unpopular as a photographer by being too close to them.

184–185. Headwaters of Spa Creek, Annapolis, Maryland, July 5, 1993

MSA SC 1890-BP-26,694

This was taken on a Sunday morning. These boats had tied up together, side by side in the creek, so that they could party Saturday night, I presume. After a race, they'll say, "Shall we raft up?" in such and such a creek, which usually means, "Shall we tie up together and party?" I was thinking as I was looking at this that a raft-up usually gets pretty noisy, and sound carries very well across the water. We're looking across here at Truxton Park, which is just woods, and I'm standing on somebody's front lawn taking this photograph. It could have been hell for the neighbors the night before with a party going on out there.

185. Camping on the Potomac River at Wynne, Maryland, August 8,

1992 MSA SC 1890-BP-25,866

I thought this was a very typical picture of life up and down the Potomac River, where people go and fish and spend the weekend or maybe their vacations there. It's a style of life on the Chesapeake.

236

When I was a child in the fifties, we began to see summer cottages being built. Folks coming down on weekends or a mother bringing her kids down to stay all summer, where the father worked in Richmond and would come down on weekends. As we began to get away from the agriculture and seafood type of economy, we began to see more changes. We haven't seen changes like Maryland has, but it's coming. LARRY CHOWNING

This isn't a particularly pretty picture, but it does make a statement about camping along the waters of the Chesapeake Bay. The lighting isn't beautiful, but it is typical. I don't think all pictures have to be done on sunny, bright days. This is a typical day on the Chesapeake. You have more days like this than you have the sunny days where you see crystal clear visions.

186–187. Chester River regatta at Love Point light, c. 1950

MSA SC 1890-MI-1600

This is the only picture I have of Love Point lighthouse. It was made during my early days on the Chesapeake, and on one of my first races, so this was a comparatively new experience for me. I was on the *Vamarie*. These boats were coming out of the Chester River to come around Kent Island and sail down to Annapolis for the finish. It was late afternoon. It had been a drifting race, meaning that there wasn't much wind. But not long after this, a summer squall came up, and we beat it home in one heck of a hurry.

Ten years later I might not have even taken this photograph because there isn't a great deal of drama to it, other than that it's backlighted, but I do think it records a weather condition that is important to photograph. Racing isn't all great sailing at top speed, making a big wake, spinnakers, and all of that. This picture records something that happens on the Bay probably more frequently than the dramatic stuff.

Love Point lighthouse has long since been torn down. There's just an electrified channel marker there now.

188. London Town Publik House, Edgewater, Maryland, March 1975

MSA SC 1890-MI-3211

There's a period of about ten minutes in which you can make night photographs on a clear evening. At that point, you still have enough light to get detail on the structure without it being just a black hole, and yet you also get the strong artificial light from the candles in the windows.

I set up here before the sun went down, and then I just waited. At the moment I judged that the daylight would be overpowered by the artificial light, I started a series of exposures. I made one, and then I waited a minute or two and made a second exposure, a third, a fourth, and maybe even a fifth, and then I said, "Well, it's too late. The shadows have gotten so dark."

In this picture, you can just make out the outline of the chimney and the roof and the cornices, and yet you have enough light to show the total outline of the building. Another five minutes after this, those chimneys would not have been visible, and all you would see would be the lights in the window.

London Town is on the South River in Edgewater. This building was a tavern at the ferry landing where colonial travelers stayed overnight. To the right of this picture is a slope that was once a rolling road where tobacco hogsheads were rolled down the hill to the water and loaded onto boats to be taken to England.

188–189. At home on the Wicomico River, Charles County, Maryland, August 7, 1992 MSA SC 1890-BP-25,805

While Mame was interviewing Etta Richwine, I wandered around her farm. I found this great massive tree and saw that I could silhouette it against the view of the Wicomico River where it meets the Potomac. And then I hit on the idea of putting Mrs. Richwine in the swing.

190–191. Point Lookout State Park, Maryland, March 30, 1968

MSA SC 1890-MI-2428-1

Point Lookout is at the very southern tip of Maryland. When you look beyond the lighthouse in the distance, you're looking out into the Chesapeake Bay. I was working for the Board of Natural Resources in those days, doing brochures for the different state parks, and this was used on the cover of a brochure for Point Lookout State Park.

In this particular case, it was very important to make this picture look different from a campground at Elk Neck State Park or one out in Garrett County. I wanted to show camping right alongside the water. This was not posed in the least; these people had no idea they were being photographed.

We were down there again recently, and we rode our bikes around. The whole campsite has been enlarged a good deal. They've got several piers to fish and crab from.

191. Friends, Kent Narrows, Maryland, May 7, 1987 MSA SC 1890-BP-21,744

I had stopped by this place just across the Bay bridge to take pictures of the migrant-worker housing nearby. I was wandering around with my camera, investigating various angles, when these two guys said, "Hey, man, take our picture!" I told them that I

would if they would get these two good-looking girls to join them. I had them pull in nice and tight and snapped this picture. Then I turned around and took the picture I really wanted.

It wasn't until I got home and made a print of this negative that I realized I had something special in the first picture, too. Each face, each smile, has a different story behind it. And, of course, I had to laugh when I saw where the guy in the middle had his hand.

192. Baiting a trotline, City Dock, Annapolis, Maryland, c. 1949

MSA SC 1890-M -12,675-1

I remember not knowing what the man here was doing and after making the picture asking him, and he said, "I'm baiting a trotline." I had to have him explain to me what a trotline was. So what he's doing is tying on a piece of eel, which would dangle in the water, and the crab would come up and start eating off of it. As he pulls it up, he will dip the crab out of the water with his net. You also see a box of Morton's Salt sitting there. Obviously he's salting down the eel to keep it from spoiling too quickly. The little wooden shovel there is used for shoveling the bait into a smaller container. It looks like there's a couple of baskets to put the crabs in.

This is a picture that I made about 1949, and I've never used it anywhere, but it's always been in the back of my mind as a picture that some day would help tell a story about crabbing.

193. Baiting a trotline, Tred Avon River, May 29, 1992

MSA SC 1890-BP-25,576

I try to include not just older people in my photographs, so here's a nice young guy baiting his trotline, and his girlfriend is riding with him. I've tried working a trotline and I get about every third crab—two of those crabs were smarter than I am, and quicker than I am. You take a good crabber and he rarely misses one. He knows when the crab's going to let go, and he's there ready for it.

Sometimes you run a trotline three or four times and you only get two or three crabs, so you pull it all back in the boat and move to another location and put it out again. Next time, you might get none, or you might get twenty crabs. I've done it when you had a crab on almost every piece of bait, and you wind up with a bushel of crabs on one run.

194. Rotary Club crab feast, Annapolis, Maryland, July 1990

MSA SC 1890-BP-24,232

Crab feasts are looked forward to the year 'round. As the crabs begin to be plentiful in the late spring, people start eating hard crabs. This is the largest crab feast in Maryland. It's conducted every year by the Rotary Club in Annapolis. They hold it under the navy stadium. It starts at five in the afternoon and usually ends about eight o'clock, when they run out of crabs.

They set up these long tables, and they attract thousands of people to the event. People come from all over. It's a big fundraiser for the Rotary Club, but it's also an opportunity to see everybody you've ever known, from politicians to neighbors. People say, "I'll see you at the Rotary Club crab feast," and if you weren't there, they'll say, "Where were you?"

The crabs are brought in by the truckload from a packer at St. Michaels. They serve more than three hundred bushels of crabs every year, a fantastic number. Along with that, you have crab soup and corn on the cob and hamburgers and hot dogs. I can eat four or five crabs, and then I want some real food, so I go get a hamburger or a hot dog or something to fill the gaps in my stomach.

195. Shucking oysters, East New Market, Maryland, December 14, 1992

MSA SC 1890-BP-26,406

In the fall there are oyster roasts, and men stand and shuck these oysters by the hundreds. People just eat them right off the shell with a little horseradish sauce and catsup. There's usually oyster stew, which is oysters cooked in milk and herbs, and there are fried oysters.

But my favorite is what they call palmed oysters, when the oysters are put in an egg batter, usually two of them together, and formed into sort of a cake. They're fried together and they're richer because it's more than one oyster. You don't get those many places.

I can remember, even in Missouri, having oysters on the half shell at restaurants. An oyster ships very well until he's opened. Back in 1932 or '33, when I was living with my father in Sikeston, Missouri, which is about as far away from the ocean as you can get, they had a lodge banquet and they served oyster stew. I'd never even heard of oyster stew, and my father tried to get me to try some. I tasted the milk, and that was as far as I would go. I would have nothing to do with it.

After we moved to Maryland, we used to go out with the legislature and they'd rent a ferry boat. They'd have beer and oysters and all kinds of food, and I think that was the first place I ever tried a raw oyster. It takes some nerve to put one of those in your mouth and swallow it. Then I had another one and, of course, a little beer to go with it, and pretty soon I liked them.

195. Shucking clams, Grasonville, Maryland, July 28, 1993

MSA SC 1890-BP-26,848

It's much easier to open a soft-shell clam than an oyster. They are made into clam chowder or fried clams, primarily. Clams absorb an awful lot off the bottom of a river. It's a healthy sign that the clams are an edible source of food. It means the water is reasonably clean. After all, there have been oyster beds and clam beds closed down on rivers that are polluted, so if they allow them to be harvested, I think there must be at least an acceptable level of purity.

196. Festival on Maryland Avenue, Annapolis, Maryland, October 3, 1992 MSA SC 1890-BP-26,106

Every fall now they have a day-long festival on Maryland Avenue. It's a challenge to take a picture there because the street runs north and south. It's lighted on one side in the morning, and the other in the afternoon. I knew that about two o'clock was the time to get the right side of the street, so I parked my van in the intersection of Prince George Street and climbed on the roof.

I wanted the food stand in the foreground because that emphasized the festival atmosphere. The price list helps to date the photograph. In ten years, the menu may change and the prices will probably be higher. I only had to wait about ten minutes for the light to be right, but then I had to wait for the crowd to form a pleasing composition. When the midshipmen walked down the street, I snapped my shutter. With them and the State House dome in the picture, you hardly have to mention Annapolis in the caption.

197. City Dock, Annapolis, Maryland, September 24, 1981

MSA SC 1890-MI-4275-7

I've done a lot of work for Historic Annapolis Foundation through the years. About 1980, they built a model of City Dock during the colonial period, and they wanted to do a present-day version, too. I convinced them that the best way to see the dock from all angles would be in aerial photographs taken from a helicopter. This is my favorite view from that particular outing. I like the strong backlighting and how clearly it shows the changes that occurred in the area in the 1970s.

198. Ice cream festival, Odenton, Maryland, July 6, 1992

MSA SC 1890-BP-25,669

A friend of mine sold me tickets to a church ice cream festival over in Odenton, and I decided it might make a good picture, so my wife and I went to it. It used to be when a lady served a piece of cake, she cut it and picked it up with her hands and put it on a napkin or plate. Well, these women all have these little plastic gloves on. Here's an old-fashioned ice cream festival with colonial costumes, and the ladies have these plastic gloves on.

The thing I hate most about this type of picture is that so many people wear these T-shirts with great fancy sayings on them, and I find those rather obnoxious. Everybody in this picture is what I would call normally dressed—and yet you could say those T-shirts are pretty normal now, too. I like to stay with what to me seems neutral editorially, but still tells a story.

This is just what I intended to do on my Bay Project—document the Chesapeake Bay and its people and how they live today. As we know from doing *Maryland Time Exposures,* half the fun of looking at historical pictures is studying the people and seeing how they dressed, or how they stood, or what they were doing. I hope my photographs will explain to people fifty years from now or a hundred years from now what life was like in the second half of the twentieth century on the Chesapeake Bay.

198–199. Somerset County Fair, Princess Anne, Maryland, 1987

MSA SC 1890-BP-22,472

I was fascinated by this row of bonnets in contrast to the hats worn by the women who were looking at them. I found it impossible to visualize these modern women in their

T-shirts and shorts wearing bonnets. My Aunt Edna, who raised me, is the last person I remember wearing a bonnet. She was a newspaper woman, but the minute she got to her farm, she put on her bonnet and long-sleeved clothes to protect herself from the sun.

Timing is everything in a picture like this. I purposely snapped the shutter as the woman reached up to the bonnet. Photographing people is difficult because you have to think it out and have the camera ready and then wait for them to do the obvious, predictable thing. Sometimes they never do it.

200–201. Remington Farms, Kent County, Maryland, c. 1963

MSA SC 1890-MI-2168 (35 mm)

Remington Farms is a private game preserve east of Chestertown in Kent County. It's open to the public. The birds seem to sense that nobody's going to shoot them on this land, so you can get fairly close to them. As it gets to be late in the afternoon, they come in and land on the pond for the night.

Feeding grasses are planted at Remington Farms to attract the birds. The game preserve gives them a refuge from the hunters and also helps to keep birds off the farmers' lands so they won't eat crops.

Birds in flight are terribly difficult to photograph because they swing in and out, and they merge, and sometimes their wings are moving so fast that they're just a blur against the skyline.

I did this on 35 mm film with a 200 mm lens, which means that I could stay a lot farther away from the birds than I could with a normal lens. I shot from my car window. If you stay in the car, even though the car is moving, it doesn't bother them, but the minute you open the door and step out, they shy away from you.

200. Remington Farms, Kent County, Maryland, c. 1970

MSA SC 1890-MI-3577 (35 mm)

I did this with a telephoto lens again from my car window. It was late in the afternoon, and the geese were coming in. These two ducks just waddled past, and I grabbed a couple of shots of them.

It's always been one of my favorites, for two reasons. One, it shows a male and a female, and they look like they belong to each other. Their heads are at the same jaunty angle. But also, the fact that they're backlighted in rather out-of-focus surroundings makes them stand out very strong.

Another thing is, they're just the right distance apart. They're not overlapping each other, but they're close enough together to be a unit. I always say that in photographing sailboats, or anything, if the things are too far apart and don't relate to one another, it's awfully hard to make a composition of it. Now, if there was another inch between them, this would be a picture of a duck here and a picture of a duck there. But when you have the two this close, it makes it a unit.

201. Hunters near Remington Farms, Kent County, Maryland, c. 1970

MSA SC 1890-MI-2590

I was invited to go goose hunting with the sports editor of the *News American* and a group of psychiatrists, and it was one of the weirdest experiences I've ever had, but that's another story. Each of these guys had his dog with him, hunting dogs, and they were so fond of their dogs that at least two of them had their dogs sleep right in the sleeping bag with them.

They bagged a number of geese the next morning, and this photograph shows two of the men, one carrying his shotgun and the other carrying two geese by the neck back up to the farmhouse where we stayed. The weather was overcast, but that's very typical of hunting. Hunters much prefer an overcast day to a bright sunny day because, I think, the geese fly better.

202. Hand-milking demonstration, Somerset County Fair, Princess Anne, Maryland, August 4, 1985 MSA SC 1890-BP-20,091

The Holstein cow here is being milked by a young man, and you can even see the squirts of milk coming into the bucket. The thing that's wonderful about this picture is the expressions on the people who are looking on. One guy is blowing a bubble with his bubble gum, and the women are sort of smiling and laughing, watching this milking, but the kids look really amazed at what's happening.

When I was a boy, I did a lot of milking and hand-milking wasn't any novelty. Now, I would say a hundred percent, or at least ninety percent, of these kids live on farms, but there are few cows in this area. And besides, hand-milking isn't done anymore; people milk by machine now.

The children today won't ever have the wonderful time that I had as a child growing up. I often have people ask me, "Do you think it's too late?" and I don't know. I don't like to think it's too late. But we've got to do more than we're doing. It's costly, it's inhibiting, but if the Chesapeake Bay is ever going to be a productive body of water again, then everybody's going to have to be a part of that solution. There's going to have to be sacrifices made. There's going to have to be greater investment.

BERNIE FOWLER

202–203. Judging livestock, Worcester County Fair, Snow Hill, Maryland, August 3, 1988 MSA SC 1890-BP-22,196

My grandchildren are very involved with the 4H Club, and I often go with them to county fairs on the lower Eastern Shore. That's where I found this girl showing her sheep. She seemed so full of pride that she caught my attention. I've noticed over the years that all the kids seem to wear white shirts when they're in the judging ring—it's almost like a uniform. These kids know that meat packers will pay a lot of money for prize-winning animals, so they've got a lot at stake when they walk into the ring.

A picture like this is really a record of how events are done today. The fences here were brought in and tied together—it's a very temporary arrangement. In the past it may have been done differently, and they'll probably figure out a better way in the future, but for right now, this is how it's done.

204. Walnut Point, Virginia, May 1986 MSA SC 1890-BP-22,729

I wandered down this country road in Virginia and found a little boatyard. These two men were talking to each other next to this boat, obviously quite relaxed and unaware that they were being photographed. They both have the baggy-pants look of older men. I suppose I should have gone up to them after I took the picture and asked, "What's your name?" "Who are you?" "What do you do?" but I've never been able to get myself to do that. What difference does it make? The names of these guys are not important to my story. The fact that they're talking alongside a boat says something about life on the Chesapeake. Who they are and even *where* they are isn't of any great consequence because I've seen this exact same scene with different people everywhere I go on the Bay.

204–205. Fishing near the mouth of the Choptank River, August 24, 1985 MSA SC 1890-BP-20,144

It's hard to make pictures of fishing from the boat you're on. Fortunately, there are usually other boats around. This boat, the *Sea Adventure* from Rockville, was one of the boats lying off alongside us. There are three people fishing off the stern and a bunch of seagulls flying around, which is very much the atmosphere of fishing in Chesapeake Bay. The day wasn't the best; there's not much shadow. They were fishing for bluefish.

206. Fishing party near the reserve fleet, James River, July 30, 1993 MSA SC 1890-BP-26,927

None of these fishermen is particularly aware of the camera. With the round stern, this is obviously a Virginia boat. You have a cooler sitting there with cold drinks in it, and a rubber tire used as a bumper. I think it's a nice picture showing a fishing party with the reserve fleet in the background.

207. Ruke's store, Ewell, Maryland, March 13, 1991 MSA SC 1890-BP-24,777

Around the Chesapeake Bay, the country store is still an important meeting place for exchanging ideas and swapping stories. Some of the stores I've visited in years past are gone now, so I'm always happy to come upon one that's still active.

I always try to make these photographs by existing light because it's more natural. Low light can be a problem for stopping action, but I try to work from a tripod and wait for a minimum of movement by my subjects. Depth of field is sometimes a problem, too; however, in this picture the background is sharp enough to show the products on the shelves. I waited long enough for these fellows to lose interest in me, and here they are obviously absorbed in their own conversation.

208. Theodore Johnson, near Annapolis, Maryland, June 26, 1992 MSA SC 1890-BP-25,743

Theodore Johnson had just turned ninety-three years old when I took his picture. I used flash on this, which is pretty obvious if you know how to recognize it. He was so black that if I hadn't used it, we wouldn't see any detail in his face at all; the only thing we'd see would be his white eyebrows and his white hair. I tried to use it as subtly as possible.

He's sitting on his porch steps, and I tried to get an angle that didn't show things that would take your eye away from him. He didn't put much importance to the fact that he was being photographed. He was more fascinated by telling his own story to Mame in their interview.

208–209. St. Mary's River, St. George Island, Maryland, August 7, 1992 MSA SC 1890-BP-25,822

Mame and I had gotten down to St. George Island late in the afternoon, and the sun was getting in a position where you could look directly at it. There were a lot of people doing surf fishing off the rocks in the St. Mary's River. This makes a nice silhouette—the boy with his net, and a younger boy with a big hat on standing quite erect, and the father—I assume it's the father—his rod is bent a little bit, which means he's got a fish on the line.

There's nothing uglier than looking at a pile of rocks. But here I'm silhouetting them, so they take on a more romantic and dramatic atmosphere than if I were doing them brightly sunlighted. Seeing the shoreline over across the river sort of helps to identify that this is a major tributary of the Chesapeake, but not the Bay itself.

210–211. Potomac River, September 20, 1985 MSA SC 1890-BP-27,131

This neck of land on the Potomac is in St. Mary's County. There's a pier coming out from a very, very narrow extent of land. The upper part is the Potomac, and the foreground is a river that flows into the Potomac. It's terribly hard when you're flying to pinpoint just where you are when you're coming up a shoreline.

I like the backlighting and the play of light on the water. There's a dark streak up in the Potomac where a boat went by sometime earlier in the day, created a turbulence, and left its track.

212–213. Skipjack on rough water, c. 1953 MSA SC 1890-MI-3543-4

Anybody who knows the Chesapeake can see that this was a very rough day. That reefed mainsail with no jib at all means that there was a pretty heavy wind out there. Still, they were out oystering. As I remember, there were a couple dozen boats out there that day, which seemed like a lot to me, but the oldtimers say there used to be a hundred at a time. Now if you see two skipjacks dredging together, it's remarkable.

213. Abandoned ferry slip at Claiborne, looking toward Kent Island, Maryland, August 11, 1963 MSA SC 1890-MI-1647B

The ferry used to go across the Bay to Romancoke and Claiborne. This was taken after the Bay bridge was built. I looked at the scene, and I saw the birds on the old pilings and the marker, and I thought, "You know, to me, that is a typical view looking out from any place on the Chesapeake Bay." You see a few pilings, you see a few markers, you see an island or a point of land off in the distance and the sun sparkling on the water.

It's a very simple photograph, meaning that there's no great excitement, but there *isn't* anything very exciting about just looking out at the Bay. It was the middle of summer and the sun was still up—it was probably about two or three o'clock in the afternoon—so you've got enough direction out of the sun without it actually being low at the horizon. It's so strongly backlighted that when I print it deep enough to get the sparkle in the water, everything grows pretty dark. It gives a sort of moonlight effect.

My wife was with me, and she criticized me when I took the picture that day. For her, there was nothing to it. After I printed it, she felt the same way. She said, "See, I told you there was nothing to that picture." But I just like the utter simplicity of it.

240. Winter morn, City Dock, Annapolis, Maryland, 1950 MSA SC 1890-MI-202B

This picture really illustrates the passage of time, because there are two bugeyes, a schooner, and two skipjacks tied up here, and they were all used for dredging oysters then. Today, there are only a few skipjacks left; no bugeyes or schooners dredge the Bay anymore.

I took this at City Dock in Annapolis, about where the Marriott Hotel is now. By necessity, it was made in the most primitive way a photograph can be. After I had trudged out in the snow and ice and gotten set up, I realized that the shutter on the lens wasn't working. I held a film holder in front of the lens, guessed at the exposure, and hoped for the best.

Winter morn, City Dock, Annapolis, Maryland, 1950

Library of Congress Cataloging-in-Publication Data

Warren, Marion E.
    Bringing Back the Bay: the Chesapeake in the photographs of Marion E. Warren
and the voices of its people / Marion E. Warren, with Mame Warren.
        p.   cm.
    ISBN 0-8018-4906-3 (alk. paper)
    1. Chesapeake Bay Region (Md. and Va.) — Pictorial works.
I. Warren, Mame, 1950-   . II. Title.
F187.C5W375   1994
975.5'18—dc20   94-18329

Designed by Gerard A. Valerio, Bookmark Studio

Composed by The Composing Room of Michigan, Inc. in Bembo text and display

Printed by the Whitmore Printing Company, Annapolis, Maryland, on 80-lb. Lithofect plus, dull

Bound by American Trade Bindery, Baltimore, Maryland, in Joanna Kennett cloth